# COLONIAL DAYS

# COLONIAL DAYS

## Discover the Past with Fun Projects, Games, Activities, and Recipes

## David C. King

John Wiley & Sons, Inc.

New York • Chichester • Weinheim • Brisbane • Singapore • Toronto

This book is printed on acid-free paper. ∞

Copyright © 1998 by Roundtable Press, Inc. and David C. King
Published by John Wiley & Sons, Inc.

A Roundtable Press Book
Directors: Marsha Melnick and Susan E. Meyer
Design concept: Barbara Hall
Design: Michaelis/Carpelis Design Assoc., Inc.

Illustrations © 1998 by Bobbie Moore

The photographs on pages 8, 82, 92, 96, and 101 are courtesy of the New York Public Library Picture Collection.

The photograph on page 30 is courtesy of the North Wind Picture Archives.

Library of Congress Cataloging-in-Publication Data
King, David C.
    Colonial Days : discover the past with fun
  projects, games, activities, and recipes / David C. King :
  illustrations by Bobbie Moore.
                              p.  cm.  —  (American kids in history ™ series)
    "A Roundtable Press book" —T.p. verso.
    Includes index.
    Summary: Discusses colonial life in America, depicts a year in the
  life of a fictional colonial family, and presents projects and
  activities, such as butter churning, candle dipping, baking bread,
  and playing colonial games.
    ISBN 0-471-16168-3 (acid-free paper)
    1. United States—Social life and customs—To 1775—Activity
  programs. 2. United States—History—Colonial period, ca.
  1600-1775—Activity programs. 3. Children—United States-
  -History— 18th century—Activity programs. 4. Children—United
  States—History—17th century—Activity programs.[1. United
  States—Social life and customs—To 1775. 2. United States-
  -History—Colonial period, ca. 1600-1775.] I. Moore, Bobbie, ill.
  II. Title. III. Series.
  E162.K58  1998
  973—dc21                                                  97—16083

Printed in the United States of America
10  9  8  7

To my father

# ACKNOWLEDGMENTS

Special thanks to the many people who made this book possible,
including: Kara N. Raezer, Joanne Palmer, and the editorial staff of the
Professional and Trade Division, John Wiley & Sons, Inc.; Susan E. Meyer and the
staff of Roundtable Press, Inc.; Marianne Palladino and Irene Carpelis of
Michaelis/Carpelis Design; Sharon Flitterman-King and Diane Ritch for craft expertise;
Rona Tuccillo for picture research; Steven Tiger, librarian, and the students of
the Roe-Jan Elementary School, Hillsdale, New York; and, for research
assistance, the staff members of the Great Barrington Public Library,
the Atheneum (Pittsfield, Massachusetts), Old Sturbridge Village, and
the Farmers Museum, Cooperstown, New York. Special thanks to
the Bidwell House (Monterey, Massachusetts)
for the photograph on page1.

# CONTENTS

# INTRODUCTION

## The Thirteen Colonies

In the early 1600s, settlers from England arrived on the shores of what is now the United States. To the newcomers, these lands were a frightening wilderness. But to the people already living here, this was home. These were the people we call the Native Americans, or American Indians. Divided into many tribes, they had been living in North America for hundreds of years. Many of the Native Americans were friendly to the first settlers. They helped the settlers survive by teaching them to plant foods that were unknown in Europe, such as corn.

After the first years of struggle, most of the settlements succeeded, and the English started more settlements. These settlements, called colonies, were ruled by England, but the colonists enjoyed far greater freedom than most people in Europe. People were willing to cross the hazardous Atlantic Ocean to what they called the "New World" to escape harsh governments, to worship as they pleased, and to start farms and trades. Some, however, came against their will. These people were captured from their homes in western Africa and forced to work as slaves, mostly on the large farms in the southern colonies, called plantations.

By the 1730s, there were thirteen English colonies in America, with a population of nearly 700,000 people. The Native Americans found themselves being crowded out by the land-hungry colonists. Some tribes fought bitter wars against the colonists for the land. Others moved west, and some tried to adopt European ways of living.

About nine out of every ten colonial families were farmers. Their farms usually were small, and they clustered around a village. Most families lived comfortably. Each farm supplied enough food for the family's needs, with some left over to sell or trade for things they wanted.

The work was hard for young and old colonists alike. By the age of nine or ten, boys worked in the fields with their fathers, and girls helped their mothers prepare meals and make clothing. In many of the colonies, boys went to school for a few weeks a year. Girls were taught at home, although some did attend schools, especially in some of the New England colonies.

## The Mayhew Family

Like most colonial families, the Mayhews were farmers. They owned a small farm on the edge of a tiny village of twelve houses called Webster's Corners in the western part of the Massachusetts colony. The Mayhew's farm supplied more than enough food for the family's needs. They took the extra crops to the larger town of Springfield, six miles away, where they traded them for things they needed.

The family's house was a modest wood frame building they built themselves with their neighbors' help. The large main room of the house, called the common room, was the center of their daily living. It served as their kitchen, dining room, living room, crafts room, and playroom. The parents had the only bedroom on the first floor. The four children shared two low-ceilinged rooms on the second floor. Heat was provided by a large stone fireplace, which was also used for cooking and baking. The chimney ran through the center of the house and opened onto small fireplaces in each of the bedrooms.

The Mayhews were not a real family, but their story shows what life was like in colonial America. This book follows the Mayhews through the year 1732.

Jonathan Mayhew, the head of the family, was descended from English colonists who had helped to establish the Massachusetts colony as a place where they would be free to worship as they pleased. His wife, Abigail Mayhew, was the daughter of a Boston sea captain and his wife. Mrs. Mayhew had known little about farming until she married Mr. Mayhew in 1719, but she quickly grew fond of their farm in the fertile valley of the Connecticut River.

Mr. Mayhew plowed and planted the farm fields and took care of the farm animals. He attended regular town meetings with his neighbors in Webster's Corners. Although Massachusetts was a colony of England, the mother country was so far away that the men of the villages and towns decided most matters for themselves. Mr. Mayhew was also a skilled carpenter, or joiner, and often worked for other people during the winter. Mrs. Mayhew managed almost everything in the household. She spent much of her time preparing food, because everything had to be made from scratch, and she made nearly all of the family's clothing by hand.

Sarah Mayhew celebrated her twelfth birthday in the spring of 1732. Her mother was teaching her how to cook and bake, how to weave wool and sew linen for clothing, how to preserve food, and how to make butter and cheese from milk. With her mother's help, Sarah was now in charge of the kitchen garden, where she grew herbs, flowers, and some vegetables.

Nathan Mayhew turned ten years old in January 1732. Like his older sister, he was learning important skills and crafts. He helped his father with plowing, planting, hoeing, and harvesting the crops. He was able to load and fire a musket, and managed to hunt small game like wild turkeys. He could also handle an ax to chop firewood and use hand tools to make things out of wood. While Sarah was taught to read and write at home, Nathan went to school for a few weeks each year.

Like all colonial children, Sarah and Nathan worked hard, but they enjoyed their work and felt great satisfaction in doing something well. They had fun on the weekly trips to market day in Springfield, when people came to trade from all the surrounding villages. They also found time for swimming, fishing, and berry picking in summer, and ice skating and snow games in winter.

Benjamin and Anne Mayhew, the youngest in the family, were twins. Although they were only five years old, they were able to help with some of the chores, like scattering feed for the chickens and geese, or searching the farmyard for freshly laid eggs.

## The Projects and Activities

What would it be like to be a kid in colonial America? In this book you'll do some of the activities that kids like Sarah and Nathan might have done in 1732. Like them, you'll churn butter, dip candles, and follow a recipe for baking bread. You'll also do some of the things colonial children did for fun, like playing jacks or making a fruit syllabub for a summertime dessert. All of the projects and activities are fun to do and use materials that you probably have at home or can easily buy at very little cost. While you won't be cooking over a stone fireplace or making your own paints out of buttermilk, you will get to do things much the way kids just like you did more than 250 years ago. As you try the activities and projects, the history of colonial America will come to life. You'll discover what it was like to be an American kid during colonial days.

# CHAPTER ONE

# SPRING

After a long, cold winter, the Mayhews were eager for the first signs of spring. They waited for the ice to break up on the Connecticut River, for the first flocks of Canadian geese flying north, and for the first warmth in a western wind. Like all farm families, their life followed the cycle of the seasons, and spring marked the beginning of the farming year.

When the ground was soft enough to plow, Mr. Mayhew hitched up the two big, sure-footed oxen and began turning over the soil. With Nathan's help, they harrowed the fields to break up the clumps of soil, then scattered seeds in the moist furrows, or rows. They planted the grains first—corn, wheat, barley, oats, and rye—along with a field of flax, the plant from which linen thread and cloth are made. They planted vegetables by a method the colonists had learned from the Indians, placing pumpkins, squash, and beans around the hills of corn.

# FARM LIFE

A variety of animals were an important part of the farm. The Mayhews raised sheep both for wool and for meat. Pigs were valuable not only for meat, but for the fat called lard, which they used for making soap. Chickens and geese provided meat and eggs, and the goose feathers were perfect for stuffing pillows, quilts, and coverlets. The two cows gave milk from spring to autumn. Mrs. Mayhew and Sarah used the milk to make butter and cheese, which could be stored for several months.

The Mayhews took some of their farm produce to a weekly market in Springfield to trade or sell. They used the money they made to buy things they could not raise or grow themselves, including gunpowder, salt, sugar, coffee, and citrus fruits, such as lemons. When there was a little extra money, they bought something made by one of the town's craftspeople—a blacksmith, potter, or seamstress. And on special occasions, they bought items like a glass window pane or a new pair of boots made in Boston or imported from England.

When the weather was too cold or wet for working in the fields, Nathan helped his father with projects in their barn workshop. They made a wooden sundial for the kitchen garden. They carved a wooden rooster for a weather vane and placed it on the peak of the barn roof. As it turned on its pole, it showed the direction the wind was blowing. By knowing the wind direction, they could figure out what the next day's weather was likely to be.

# PROJECT  MODEL WEATHER VANE

Most colonial weather vanes were either carved from wood or made by a blacksmith out of cast iron. The shapes were simple, with roosters, cows, and other farm animals being the most popular in farming areas. Weather vanes in coastal towns were likely to be shaped like a fish, whale, or sailing ship. You'll make your model weather vane out of poster board. You can copy one of the traditional colonial shapes and make a clay stand for displaying your model.

## MATERIALS

*several sheets of newspaper*
*pencil*
*ruler*
*poster board, about 10 inches square*
*scissors*
*reddish brown crayon*
*black felt-tip pen, fine point*
*½ pound self-hardening clay*
*unsharpened pencil*
*cellophane tape*

**1.** Cover your work area with newspaper.

**2.** Use the pencil and ruler to copy one of the traditional colonial weather vane shapes on the poster board. The horse should measure about

7 inches from the forward hoof to the tail and 5 inches high; the cow should measure about 7 inches by 4 inches; and the rooster should measure 5 inches from beak to tail and 6 inches high.

**3.** Cut out the weather vane shape.

**4.** Use a reddish brown crayon to color the model vane lightly on both sides. Add details, such as an eye or feather lines on the rooster with the felt-tip pen.

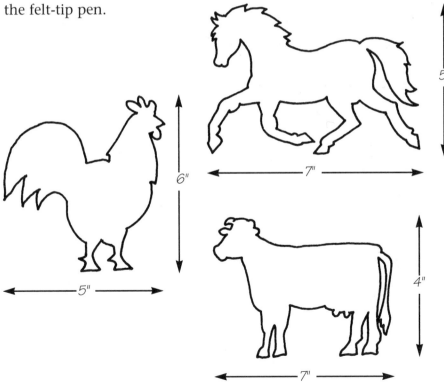

# Weather Vane Symbols

During the Middle Ages, the Catholic Church decreed that the symbol of a rooster should be placed on top of every church steeple in Europe as a sign of Christian faith. The fish was also an early Christian symbol. The colonists brought these symbols to the New World and adopted them for their weather vanes.

Although the rooster, fish, and horse were the most popular shapes, the colonists made vanes in an amazing variety of forms, including angels, grasshoppers, sea serpents, and the symbols of various trades and crafts.

**5.** Remove the self-hardening clay from the package. Knead the clay for a few minutes to make it soft. Break off enough clay to make a stand for the weather vane about 4 inches wide, 2 inches long, and 2 inches high.

**6.** With the unsharpened pencil, make a hole in the center of the stand. Push the pencil all the way through the stand and make the hole large enough for the pencil to turn freely. Allow the clay to harden according to the directions on the package, usually 2 to 3 hours.

**7.** After the clay has hardened, color the stand with the reddish brown crayon.

**8.** Tape your poster board weather vane to one end of the pencil and insert the other end in the hole in the stand.

**9.** Try your weather vane outdoors. Place the stand on any level surface. The vane will turn in the breeze and point in the direction the wind is blowing.

SUNDIAL

Many colonial families could afford to buy a clock in the 1730s, but sundials remained popular as garden timepieces, and they are still common today. Sundials consist of an upright part (called a gnomon) and a flat surface. The gnomon's shadow on the surface shows the time of day.

Most colonial sundials were made of copper, which aged to a grayish green color. You can make your sundial out of poster board and create the look of aged copper with acrylic or poster paints. Display your sundial indoors and, on bright or sunny days, use it outdoors to see how accurately it keeps track of time.

## MATERIALS
*several sheets of newspaper*
*drawing compass*
*11-inch-square piece of 1/2-inch-thick wood or stiff*
   *cardboard*
*pencil*
*ruler*
*piece of poster board or cardboard about*
   *8 x 12 inches*
*scissors*
*small plastic dish*
*acrylic paints or poster paints: light gray, green, white*
*medium paintbrush*

*black felt-tip pen, fine point*
*white glue*
*directional compass*
*watch or clock*

**1.** Cover your work area with newspaper.

**2.** Use the drawing compass to draw a circle on the 11-inch-square piece of wood or cardboard. The circle should measure 10 inches in diameter (length of a straight line through the center of the circle). Set aside.

**3.** To make the gnomon (the upright part of a sundial), use the pencil and ruler to draw a 5-inch-by-5-inch-by-7-inch triangle on the piece of poster board or cardboard as shown on the following page. Cut out the gnomon.

**4.** Make two braces to hold the gnomon upright. On the remaining posterboard, measure and mark with the pencil two rectangles, each 4 inches long and about 2 inches wide.

**5.** Cut out the two rectangles and fold them in half the long way, as shown in the picture.

Braces for gnomon

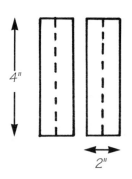

4"

2"

Gnomon

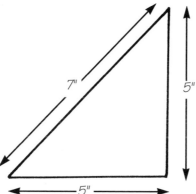

7"

5"

5"

Face of the Sundial

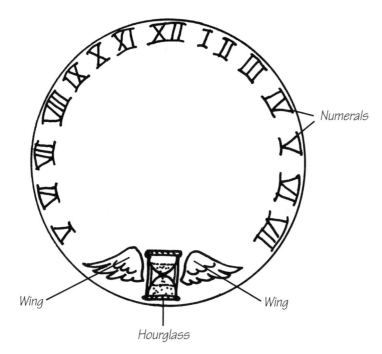

Numerals

Wing

Hourglass

Wing

**6.** To give the sundial the weathered copper look, mix some light gray paint with green on the plastic dish. If the color looks too dark, add a little white paint.

**7.** When you're satisfied with the color, take the piece of wood or cardboard you set aside in step 1. This will be the face of the sundial. Paint the circle face as well as the gnomon and the two braces. Allow the paint to dry for about 1 hour.

**8.** With pencil, copy the numbers and the drawing shown in the picture onto the circle face. (Notice that the numbers are arranged differently from the face of a clock.)

**9.** Using the felt-tip pen, carefully go over the numerals, the hourglass, and the wings. Go over the outline of the circle in black as well.

**10.** Position the gnomon on the face of the sundial, with the point of the triangle in the center of the circle, and the side of the triangle pointing toward the XII, as shown.

**11.** Spread glue on the sides of the braces that will touch the gnomon and circle face. Place one brace on each side of the gnomon. Press against

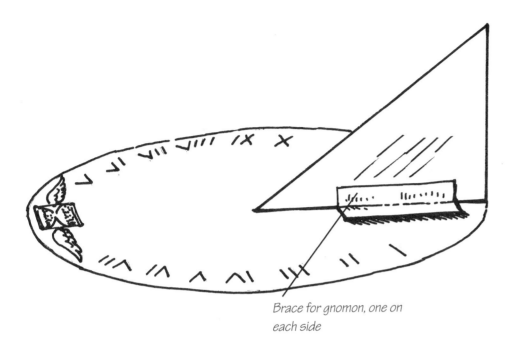

Brace for gnomon, one on each side

the gnomon and the circle face to hold the gnomon upright. Allow the glue to dry.

**12.** On a sunny or bright day, place your sundial on a flat surface outdoors. Use the directional compass to find south. Position the sundial so that the highest part of the gnomon points south. Use the watch or clock to check the correct time. Now turn the sundial until the gnomon's shadow falls on that time. Check your sundial every half hour or hour. How well does it keep the time?

# The March of Time

Clocks as we know them today were fairly new when the colonies were established. The first real clocks were invented in the 1500s. By the early 1700s, there were a number of outstanding clockmakers in the colonies, especially around Boston and in Connecticut. Colonial clockmakers were usually highly skilled cabinetmakers, who also made remarkably accurate clocks.

# EARLY HARVEST

Warmer days in early March meant the Mayhews could tap the maple trees for sap to make into maple syrup. Sarah and Nathan made spouts, called spiles, by hollowing out pieces of branch from the red-berried sumac tree. Their father drilled holes in the towering maple trees, tapped in the spiles, and hung wooden buckets to catch the dripping sap.

Within a few days, they had collected enough sap to start boiling it down. Nathan hauled firewood, Mrs. Mayhew tended the outdoor fire under a big iron kettle, and Sarah skimmed foam off the top. By the time they had finished, Mr. Mayhew figured they had collected more than 200 gallons of sap. When they boiled it down, they had 22 quarts of pure maple syrup sealed in pottery jugs. For Sarah, Nathan, and the twins, the best part of the work came when they were allowed to use some of the syrup for treats like Jack Wax and maple cream candy.

In addition to making maple syrup, warmer weather allowed the family to add to their food supply in other ways. Sarah and her mother could now start growing the first herb seeds indoors for transplanting later into the kitchen garden. They also gathered wild plants, including dandelions, which they ate as a steamed vegetable or in salad. Sometimes they brewed the dandelion blossoms as a tea.

# PROJECT DANDELION SALAD

Today most Americans think of dandelions as troublesome weeds. Since colonial times, however, many people have found that they are a delicious food, especially in a salad. Plus, they're packed with vitamins A and C.

When you pick dandelions, look for the youngest leaves for the best taste, and make sure you're in an area that has not been sprayed with chemicals. You can pick dandelions throughout their growing season, but springtime is best.

## INGREDIENTS

*1 small clove of garlic*
*5 tablespoons vinegar*
*2 teaspoons sugar*
*1/4 teaspoon pepper*
*about 2 pounds fresh-picked dandelion greens*
*1 hard-boiled egg*
*2 or 3 small scallions*
*1 tomato*
*salt and pepper*

## EQUIPMENT

*paring knife*
*cutting board*
*mixing bowl*
*wooden spoon*
*colander*
*paper towels*
*serving bowl*
*fork*
*mixing spoon*
*salad tongs or two serving spoons*
*adult helper*

## MAKES
*about 4 servings*

**1.** Ask an adult to help you use the paring knife to cut the garlic clove into tiny pieces on the cutting board.

**2.** Place the garlic pieces in the mixing bowl. Add the vinegar, sugar, and pepper and stir well with the wooden spoon. Allow the mixture to stand for about 30 minutes.

**3.** While the mixture is standing, trim the dandelion greens by cutting off the stems of the leaves. Discard any blossoms. Wash and strain the leaves in the colander and pat them dry with paper towels.

# The Incredible Edible Cattail

Cattails are tall swamp plants with a brown, sausage-like seed head. One of the lessons the Native Americans taught the colonists was that almost every part of the American species of cattail is edible, or can be used in some other way. The leaves are the only part that can't be eaten, but the Native Americans and colonists used these for weaving baskets and mats.

The colonists harvested cattails for different foods in each season of the year. Even in winter, they dug up the underground stems, peeled off the husk, and used the stems as a potato substitute or ground them into flour. (An acre of cattails produces more flour than the same acre of wheat.)

**4.** Have the adult help you use the paring knife to mince (cut into very small pieces) the hard-boiled egg, scallions, and tomato. Set aside.

**5.** Place the dandelion greens in the serving bowl and add the vinegar-sugar-garlic mixture. Mix thoroughly with a fork and mixing spoon.

**6.** Sprinkle the minced egg, scallions, and tomato on top of the salad. Salt and pepper to taste. Toss the salad with the salad tongs or serving spoons and serve.

# PROJECT INDOOR HERB GARDEN

If you have never planted a garden before, growing herbs is a perfect way to start. Herbs are easy to grow. They produce useful plants in just a few weeks, and most will stay around even if you forget to water them on time.

Herbs are especially fun for indoor gardening because you can grow them throughout the year and watch their progress closely. Chives, dill, and parsley are good for cooking or for salads, and you might want to grow some lavender or lemon balm for making potpourri or a sachet (see Chapter 2). You also can dry the herbs for later use. Keep chives by putting them in a plastic bag and storing them in the freezer.

## MATERIALS

*several sheets of newspaper*
*small pail of sand*
*small bag of potting soil (available at garden centers,*
    *discount department stores, and most supermarkets)*
*a few handfuls of pebbles or gravel*
*4 or 5 small flowerpots with saucers, or 1 planter*
    *about 4 inches wide and 12 inches long (You can*
    *substitute paper or plastic cups for the flower pots,*
    *but place them in a box to prevent spills.)*
*gardening trowel or an old mixing spoon*
*seeds for 4 or 5 different herbs: chives, parsley,*
    *lavender, sage, thyme, or lemon balm*

*4 or 5 craft sticks*
*marking pen*

**1.** Spread newspaper on your work surface. On the newspaper mix 1 part sand with 3 parts potting soil. (Herb plants grow best in a sandy soil that drains well.) Make enough of this mixture to fill your 4 or 5 pots or planter.

**2.** Place a small handful of pebbles or gravel in the bottom of the pots. (About 1 inch of pebbles is enough.)

**3.** Use the trowel or old mixing spoon to put the soil on top of the pebbles in each pot. Pack the soil down lightly. Fill each pot to about 1/2 inch from the top.

**4.** Plant the seeds according to the directions on the seed packets. Put only one kind of herb seed in each container. (If you use a planter, give each plant 4 to 6 inches of space for growing.)

**5.** Write the name of each herb on a craft stick with the marking pen and put it in the container. (If you use a planter, place each stick adjacent to the spot where you planted the seed.)

# Herbs as Medicines

The colonists not only used herbs for cooking, but they also learned from the Native Americans how to use them as medicines. For example, for sore throats or coughs colonial women made comfrey root, rosemary, or chamomile into a hot tea with honey and lemon. They used feverfew to take the sting out of insect bites and to repel mosquitoes. They mixed comfrey root and marshmallow to make a soothing ointment for burns, and used jewelweed to remove the itch of poison ivy or poison oak.

Some colonists thought garlic was useful for headaches, earaches, and upset stomach, while peppermint tea was recommended for someone who felt depressed. In larger towns and cities, apothecary shops sold a wide variety of herbal medicines. Apothecaries were the earliest form of drugstores.

**6.** Place the pots in a sunny location. Most herbs need about 6 hours of direct sunlight every day. Water them according to the directions on the packets. The soil should always be slightly moist, especially on days when the sun is very bright.

**7.** Turn the containers or planter every two or three days so the plants receive even exposure to the sun and will then grow evenly. (Some seeds take up to two weeks to germinate, or start, so don't worry if no green shoots appear right away.)

**8.** When the plants are about 5 inches tall, pinch off the tops. This will make them bushier.

**9.** Cut kitchen herbs, like parsley and chives, whenever they are tall enough to be used for cooking or in salads. After two or three months, you can cut the plants back almost to the soil line and they will start over, giving you several more crops.

 **JACK WAX**

The last step in making maple syrup is called sugaring off, when the syrup goes through its final cooking. For colonial children, one of the rewards of maple sugaring was being allowed to pour some of the hot syrup over a bowl of fresh snow. They called this simple dish by different names: Jack Wax, sugar-on-snow, and maple snow. To make this yourself, the only ingredients you need are clean, fresh snow (or crushed ice) and maple syrup. Make sure you use pure maple syrup. Some of the imitation syrups sold in supermarkets will not work very well.

### INGREDIENTS
*2 cups pure maple syrup*
*fresh, clean snow or crushed ice, enough to fill 3 small bowls*

### EQUIPMENT
*saucepan*
*mixing spoon*
*3 bowls*
*3 spoons*
*candy thermometer*
*adult helper*

### MAKES
*about 3 servings*

# Trading Maple Syrup Ideas

When the first European colonists arrived on the North American coast, they were surprised to see Native Americans drawing sap from the maple trees. The Europeans had never seen anything like it, and they called the sap "maple water." The Native Americans poured the sap into troughs made of hollow logs and heated it by dropping hot stones into the trough.

The colonists quickly learned how valuable maple syrup could be, especially because sugar had to be imported from the West Indies. They improved on the Native American methods by boiling the sap to higher temperatures in large iron kettles, and by straining it. The Native Americans, in turn, borrowed these ideas, and the Europeans' iron kettles became a favorite trade item. Maple syrup today is still produced only in the United States and Canada.

**1.** Ask an adult helper to heat the maple syrup in a saucepan over medium heat.

**2.** While the syrup is heating, use the mixing spoon to pack the 3 bowls firmly with fresh snow or crushed ice.

**3.** Have the adult use the candy thermometer to check the heat of the syrup. When the temperature reaches 230°F, have the adult help you pour it over the snow or ice.

**4.** The hot syrup on the cold snow or ice creates a candy that is very much like taffy. Eat it with spoons!

 **MAPLE CREAM**

Maple cream was another favorite of colonial children, and it's as easy to make as Jack Wax. You can eat it like fudge, or crumble some on top of fruit, cereal, or ice cream.

### INGREDIENTS
*2 cups pure maple syrup*
*1 tablespoon butter*

### EQUIPMENT
*saucepan*
*candy thermometer*
*wooden mixing spoon*
*table knife*
*wax paper*
*adult helper*

### MAKES
*2 cups candy or topping*

**1.** Pour the maple syrup into the saucepan.

**2.** Have an adult heat the syrup on the stove at medium heat to 239°F, using the candy thermometer to check the temperature.

**3.** Turn off the heat and immediately begin beating the syrup with the wooden mixing spoon. Keep stirring hard until the syrup hardens into a smooth candy, like fudge.

**4.** Use the table knife or your fingers to spread the butter on a sheet of wax paper. Spoon the maple cream onto the wax paper.

**5.** Cut the maple cream into 1-inch squares and serve.

# SPRINGTIME ACTIVITIES

The Mayhews gathered wild plants not only for food but also for dyeing wool and linen. They used the bark of the black oak to make a bright yellow dye bath. Onion skins made a softer yellow. The family experimented with flowers, nuts, berries, twigs, roots, and leaves to produce a rainbow of rich hues. After dyeing the wool different colors, Sarah chose her favorites to begin weaving a bedspread called a coverlet for her little sister Anne's bed.

During the dyeing work, Mrs. Mayhew's brother, Samuel Cook, arrived from Boston for a long visit. Uncle Samuel was a sea captain who had just returned from nearly two years at sea. Sarah and Nathan were delighted to see their uncle and to hear his sea stories. He showed Nathan how shipbuilders measured the height of trees to be used for ship's masts.

Among the gifts he brought were pineapples, and he showed the children how to grow their own. He explained to Nathan and Sarah that when a sea captain returned from a voyage, he stuck a pineapple on a gate post as a sign that he was home and visitors were welcome. Pineapples came from distant ports in South America and the Hawaiian Islands. They became a favorite colonial symbol for hospitality and welcome. Nathan tried putting one on a post, but a raccoon thought it was meant for him and made off with it.

## PROJECT GROWING A PINEAPPLE

Because the colonists were so fond of pineapples and citrus fruits like oranges, lemons, and limes, they often tried to grow them indoors. These warm-climate plants made attractive houseplants, but they never seemed to bear fruit—except for the pineapple. Sometimes, if you're lucky, your pineapple will produce small fruits, but only after a couple of years. Even without the fruit, pineapples are easy to plant and fun to watch grow. With regular watering, the plant will last three or four years.

### MATERIALS

*several sheets of newspaper*
*carving knife (to be handled only by an adult)*
*pineapple top*
*flowerpot*
*small pail of sand*
*potting soil*
*paint stir-stick or piece of doweling*
*watering can filled with tap water*
*adult helper*

**1.** Spread newspaper over your work surface.

**2.** Have the adult use the carving knife to cut off the top of the pineapple. (The leaves should not be separated from the top.) Place the top on its side and allow it to dry for about 1 week.

## Name Change

In 1492, when Christopher Columbus landed on islands in the Caribbean Sea, he thought they were the islands off the coast of Asia known as the Indies. Because of this mistake, he called the people living on the islands "Indians." The name was later applied to all the Native American peoples living in North and South America.

Christopher Columbus was also the first European to taste what he called "Indian pinecones." The name was later changed to "pineapple," maybe from the Dutch word for pinecone, which is *pi jnappel*. In the 1700s, colonial and European traders spread pineapple growing to Africa, southern Asia, and the Pacific islands, including Hawaii.

**3.** When the top is dry, fill the flowerpot with about 3 parts sand and 1 part potting soil. Mix the sand and soil thoroughly with a stir-stick or dowel.

**4.** Pour enough water into the pot to moisten the sandy soil.

**5.** Plant the top of the pineapple deep enough so that only the leaves can be seen.

**6.** Place the pot in a warm place where it will get plenty of direct sunlight. Keep the soil moist by watering every 2 to 3 days. After about two to three months (60 to 90 days), the roots will be well formed. At that time, you can transplant your pineapple to a pot of soil without sand. Continue to water twice a week.

 **MEASURING TREE HEIGHT**

Before cutting down a tree to use for a ship's mast or to sell for lumber, the colonists estimated the height of the tree to make sure it was the size they needed. Working outdoors with a partner, you can use the same method to measure the height of any tree or building.

**MATERIALS**
*tape measure or yardstick*
*ball of string*
*scissors*
*tree*
*pole or long straight stick*
*helper*

**1.** Use the tape measure or yardstick to measure a piece of string 60 feet long. Cut the string.

**2.** Have your helper hold the string at the base of the tree, while you stretch out the string to the distance of 60 feet from the tree. Place the pole or stick in the ground at that point.

**3.** While your helper holds the pole straight up, use the tape measure to measure another 6 feet from the tree, starting at the pole.

**4.** Lie down with your head at the 6-foot point and your feet pointing toward the pole and tree. Your head will be 6 feet from the pole and 66 feet from the tree.

**5.** Keep your head as close to the ground as you can and look past the pole to the top of the tree. You will see the top of the tree somewhere along the pole. Have your helper move his or her hand up or down the pole to mark the point on the pole where you see the top of the tree.

**6.** Measure the distance on the pole from the ground to your helper's hand. Multiply that distance by 10 to get the tree's height. Example: If your helper's hand is 34 inches from the ground, the tree is 340 inches tall, or a little more than 28 feet.

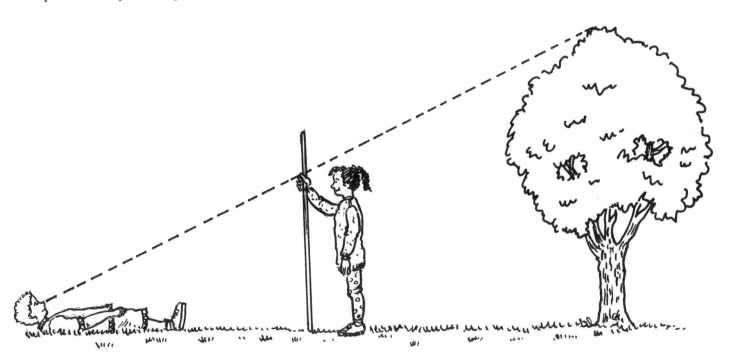

# PROJECT DYEING WOOL

Most colonial kids enjoyed dyeing wool and trying to guess what shade and color would come out of that day's dye bath. Of course, the fun of dyeing came only after they had spent long hours carding the wool (straightening the fibers with a stiff wire brush) and then spinning it into yarn.

You can use any light-colored or white yarn for dyeing. Just as colonial kids did, you'll use onion skins for the dye. Yellow onions produce a color ranging from deep yellow to burnt orange, while red onions make a reddish-brown dye.

You'll follow four basic steps: (1) washing the yarn, called scouring; (2) adding a mordant (a chemical that helps to fix the dye and keep it from running); (3) making the dye bath; and (4) dyeing the yarn. As you work, handle the yarn gently; don't touch it any more than necessary. When you've finished, save the yarn for the next project.

## MATERIALS

*1 skein of wool yarn, white or any light color (Acrylic yarn may be used if yarn made of real wool can't be found.)*
*4 short pieces of string*
*pair of rubber gloves*
*4-gallon enamel or stainless steel cooking pot (The kind used for canning is perfect.)*
*tap water*
*large wooden spoon or a 2-foot piece of doweling*
*2 ounces neutral laundry soap, such as Ivory Flakes or Woolite*
*3 ounces alum (available at supermarkets)*
*1 ounce cream of tartar*
*hand towel*
*6 to 8 cups red or yellow onion skins (only the dry outer skins)*
*cheesecloth, about 24 inches square, or a colander*
*1- or 2-quart cooking pot (optional)*
*adult helper*

**1.** To keep the yarn from getting tangled, it's helpful to keep it on the skein (the coiled roll). Do this by tying 3 of the string pieces around it very loosely.

**2.** Put on the rubber gloves. Fill the 4-gallon pot with warm tap water (not hot). Use the wooden spoon to stir in the soap flakes.

**3.** Put the yarn in the pot and let it soak for 15 minutes.

**4.** Wash the yarn gently by squeezing the suds through the yarn with your hands, then rinse the yarn in warm running water until all traces of soap are gone.

**5.** Dump the soapy water out of the pot and fill it about halfway with lukewarm tap water.

**6.** Stir in the alum and cream of tartar until dissolved. This is the mordant bath.

**7.** Add the wet yarn to the mordant bath, and ask your adult helper to bring the water to a simmer over a stove burner. Simmer for about 30 minutes, using the wooden spoon to keep the yarn under water.

**8.** Have the adult turn off the heat. Allow the yarn to cool in the pot for about 15 minutes.

**9.** When the yarn is cool, rinse it in lukewarm tap water. Gently squeeze the rinse water from the yarn (don't wring the yarn), and place it on a towel. Dump out the rinse water from the pot.

**10.** To make the dye bath, place the onion skins in a piece of cheesecloth and tie up the corners with the remaining piece of string to make a bag. (If you don't have cheesecloth, put the loose onion skins into the pot and use a large strainer later.)

**11.** Place the cheesecloth bag in the pot and add enough tap water to cover the onion skins. Have the adult bring the pot to a simmer and cook for 20 minutes. Add more water to the pot if necessary to keep the onion skins covered.

## Eliza's Prize

In 1739, Eliza Lucas's father was sent to the West Indies to serve in a government post. Sixteen-year-old Eliza was placed in charge of her family's three South Carolina plantations. Not only did young Eliza manage the plantations, but she also spent nearly four years experimenting with indigo, a West Indies plant that was prized for its rich blue dye. She finally managed to develop a variety that would survive the inland Southern summers, which are hotter than the West Indies climate that indigo usually grows in.

Thanks to Eliza, indigo became an important crop, and the famous blue dye was available at much lower cost throughout the colonies. A few years later, Eliza married Charles Pinckney and raised a family. Her two sons became heroes in the American Revolution (1775–1783), the war against England that resulted in independence for the colonies. Later, Eliza's sons helped form the government of the new nation.

**12.** After 20 minutes, have the adult turn off the heat. Remove the cheesecloth bag (with the onion skins in it) and discard it. (If you haven't used cheesecloth, have the adult help you pour the dye bath through a strainer into a smaller pot. After straining, pour the dye bath back into the 4-gallon pot.)

**13.** To dye the yarn, add enough cold water to the dye bath to fill the pot about 3/4 full. (This makes a dye bath solution of about 3 gallons.).

**14.** Put the wool in the dye bath and ask the adult to slowly bring it to a simmer. Simmer for 20 to 30 minutes, or until the yarn takes on a

shade you like. Keep in mind that the color will be lighter when the yarn dries.

**15.** Have the adult turn off the heat. Let the yarn cool in the pot for at least another 20 minutes.

**16.** Rinse the yarn thoroughly in cool running water. When the rinse water runs clear, the rinse is completed.

**17.** Gently squeeze out the water, untie the strings holding the yarn, and hang the yarn to dry away from direct sunlight. Allow 2 to 3 days for the yarn to dry completely.

## PROJECT WEAVING A POT HOLDER

Colonial girls and their mothers spent many hours weaving wool and linen thread into cloth. They made clothing for the family, as well as coverlets, linen towels, and other fabric items. Weaving was done on a wooden frame, or loom. Warp threads were stretched tightly on the frame for a base, then weft threads were woven in and out of the warp. You can make your own loom out of cardboard. The pot holder you make in this activity can be used under hot dishes, and it makes an attractive gift.

### MATERIALS
*pencil*
*ruler*
*stiff cardboard, about 10 x 12 inches*
*scissors*
*1 to 2 yards medium- or heavy-weight yellow yarn or*
  *yarn from the previous project*
*Scotch tape*
*1 to 2 yards medium- or heavy-weight blue yarn*
*craft stick or tongue depressor*
*comb with widely spaced teeth (optional)*

**1.** To make the loom:
**a.** Use the pencil and ruler to draw a line 1/2 inch in from 10-inch side of the piece of cardboard.

**b.** Make a dot every 1/2 inch along the two lines.

**c.** Use the scissors to cut v-shaped notches on both ends of the cardboard. The bottom of each v should be on the 1/2-inch dots, as shown in the drawing.

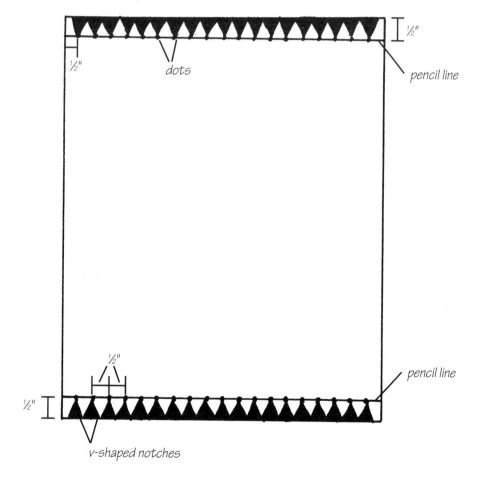

Cut away shaded sides

½"

½"    dots

pencil line

½"

½"

pencil line

v-shaped notches

**2.** To make the warp thread:

**a.** Tape one end of the yellow yarn to the back of the loom, in the center.

**b.** Wind this warp thread across the front of the loom and hook it over the top left end notch.

**c.** Run the thread down the length of the loom to the opposite left notch. Hook it around that notch and go back up to the second notch at the top.

**d.** Continue until you have hooked over all the notches. As you wind the warp from notch to notch, pull it quite tight. (If you run out of yarn, simply tie on another piece in the same color or in a different color.)

**e.** When you finish the warp, the end will be at the opposite corner from the beginning. Carry the end to the back of the board and tie it firmly to the beginning thread.

**3.** Tape one end of the blue yarn to a craft stick. This will be your shuttle, which is used to weave the weft thread.

**4.** To weave, start at either of the 12-inch sides and as close as possible to one of the rows of notches. This will be the top of the loom. Run the shuttle under the first warp thread, over the second, under the third, and so on all the way across.

**5.** When you have finished the first row, push the blue weft thread snugly toward the top of the loom. As you weave more rows, you can use the comb to push the woven threads up to keep the weaving even.

**6.** To start the second row of weaving, turn the shuttle around, and go back the other way, going over and under in the opposite way from the previous row. In other words, where you went under a warp thread in row 1, you'll go over it in row 2. Note: Don't pull the blue weft threads as tightly as you did the warp. In fact, you can make a little loop as you turn to start a new row. If you see the yellow warp threads being tugged toward the middle, you'll know that your blue threads are too tight.

**7.** When the weaving is finished, remove the tape from the tail end of the weft thread on the back of the loom and weave it in toward the center.

**8.** Remove the weaving from the loom by lifting the yellow warp threads off the notches.

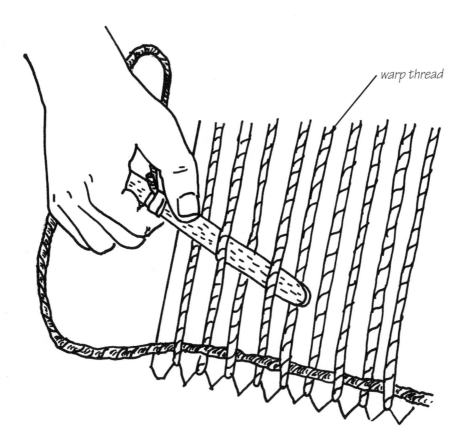

*warp thread*

# The Importance of Weaving

Wealthy colonists bought cotton, wool, and linen fabric from England, but most colonial families made their own. The weaving of cloth was so important that in 1640 Massachusetts passed a law stating that every family had to produce a certain amount of cotton each year or pay a heavy fine.

By the early 1700s, many men as well as women had become professional weavers. Some set up shops, while others became journeymen, traveling from village to village. Young boys and girls were hired as apprentices to learn the craft.

**9.** To complete the weaving, cut the ends of the yellow warp threads and tie each end in a knot close to each end row of weaving.

**10.** For hanging, cut a 4-inch piece of yarn and tie it to a corner of the pot holder.

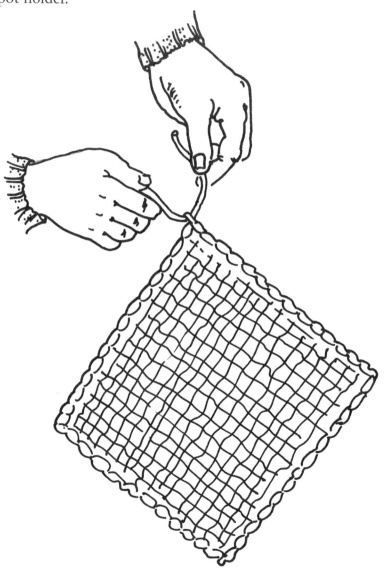

# CHAPTER TWO

# SUMMER

Early in the summer, the Mayhews said good-bye to Uncle Samuel as he set off again for Boston to prepare for his next voyage. By this time, the family was enjoying the first harvest of the year. They cut the hay and stored it in the barn to provide feed for the animals through the late autumn and winter. Sarah tended the kitchen garden carefully and was delighted when she could pick the first early carrots and lettuce.

Sarah and Nathan took Benjamin and Anne on berry-picking trips. They filled their baskets with wild strawberries, and a few weeks later, they picked raspberries and blueberries. Sarah helped her mother use some of the fruit to make jams, jellies, and preserves. They also dried some of the fruit and rolled it into sheets of oiled cloth for storage. During the winter, Mrs. Mayhew would use the dried fruit to bake pies.

# HERBS AND FLOWERS

Throughout the summer and autumn, Sarah harvested some of the herbs she had grown, and Nathan helped her search for wild herbs and flowers. They tied the herbs and a few flowers in bunches and hung them from beams in the kitchen to dry. Mrs. Mayhew taught Sarah many different ways to use the dried plants. They mixed wild rose petals with water and used the rose water for cooking and as a soothing skin lotion. Mrs. Mayhew showed Sarah how to use some herbs for medicines, and others, like dill, savory, and thyme, to add flavor to recipes.

The Mayhews also preserved the scent of dried herbs and flowers. They put the petals in jars or open dishes as potpourri and in small cloth bags called sachets. The sachets and potpourris gave every room of the house a pleasant aroma, even during the winter. Like the other colonists, the Mayhews believed that the dried herbs and flowers were good for their health, too. They knew nothing about viruses or germs, so they thought that foul odors could cause some diseases. By sweetening the air with sachets and potpourris, Mrs. Mayhew hoped that everyone in the family could avoid serious winter illnesses.

## PROJECT POTPOURRI

Today we have modern spray cans for sweetening the air, but many people still prefer the potpourris (mixtures of dried herbs, petals, and spices) that the colonists used. Almost any combination of herb leaves and flower petals will produce a wonderful scent, and part of the fun is experimenting with different mixtures. You can use herbs you've grown yourself, or, with adult permission, pick some garden herbs and a few flower blossoms. You can also buy herbs and flowers at supermarkets and garden stores, or ask a florist for blossoms that are being thrown away.

Use two or three different kinds of herbs, such as lavender, rosemary, lemon verbena, or mint. Two or three kinds of flower petals will add color as well as aroma. The blossoms of roses, geraniums, marigolds, violets, and hollyhocks work well. With adult permission, you can add some kitchen spices, too. The scent of your potpourri will last longer if you add a fixative (an ingredient that "holds" the scent), like ground orrisroot (available at natural food stores, some supermarkets, and craft stores) or a scented oil, like sandalwood oil or rose essence.

**MATERIALS**

*several sheets of newspaper*

*15 to 20 flower blossoms from one or more of the following: roses, geraniums, marigolds, violets, hollyhocks*

*25 to 30 herb leaves with branches from one or more of the following: lavender, rosemary, lemon verbena, mint (enough to fill 6 to 8 cups)*

*large mixing spoon*

*fruit and vegetable peeler*

*1 lemon or orange*

*spices: 4 tablespoons whole cloves*

*2 cinnamon sticks or 3 tablespoons ground cinnamon*

*2 teaspoons ground orrisroot or 1 teaspoon scented oil*

*4 small jars with lids (either glass or plastic)*

*3 small dishes or teacups (optional)*

**1.** Spread several sheets of newspaper in a warm, dry location away from direct sunlight where they can remain undisturbed for several days.

**2.** Pick the petals off the flower blossoms and the leaves off the herbs. Spread the material on the newspaper. Use the peeler to add a few pieces of lemon or orange rind.

**3.** Allow the petals and leaves to dry for 8 to 10 days. Use a mixing spoon to stir the material once or twice a day. When the petals and leaves feel dry and crisp, they are ready to use.

**4.** Divide the dry plant material into 4 separate piles.

**5.** Experiment to give each pile a different scent by shifting some of the different ingredients from one pile to another. Add spices and/or pieces of lemon or orange rind to change the scents. Here are three possible combinations:

**a.** For a refreshing flower-blossom scent, use lots of flower petals and lavender. Add 4 or 5 pieces of lemon or orange rind.

**b.** For a minty or citrus aroma, use mint leaves, if you have them, and geranium, rosemary, and lemon rind.

**c.** For a spicy, outdoorsy aroma, add the whole cloves and lemon or orange rind. Break up the cinnamon sticks into small pieces and add them.

**6.** When you are satisfied with your four mixtures, add 1/2 teaspoon of ground orrisroot or a few drops of scented oil to each pile. Stir to mix it in.

**7.** Put each pile into a jar. Tighten the lids on the jars and store them in a cool, dry place for 2 weeks. Shake the jars every day or so to mix the ingredients.

**8.** After the mixtures have aged for 2 weeks, use 3 of the jars for potpourri and save one jar for making sachets in the next project.

**9.** Leave the potpourris in the jars, with the lids off, or pour the mixtures into small dishes or teacups. Place each potpourri in a different room and enjoy your colonial-style air fresheners.

# The Pot That Rots

Potpourri was originally made as a moist mixture of petals and leaves that was allowed to ferment, or stew, in a crock for several months. In French, this stewing method was called potpourri, meaning "rotten pot." The word is often used today to mean any combination of items.

 **SACHET**

Sachets are a great way to add a pleasant scent to storage chests, closet shelves, and dresser drawers. Tuck your sachets in out-of-the-way corners and the aroma will remain active for a year or more.

**MATERIALS**

*several sheets of newspaper*
*2 cups potpourri from the previous project*
*four 9-inch-square pieces of lightweight cotton*
*    fabric, solid color or prints (available at fabric*
*    stores or discount department stores)*
*measuring cup*
*scissors*
*4 pieces of string, each about 6 inches long*
*4 pieces of narrow ribbon, each about 8 inches long*

**1.** Spread the newspaper on your work surface. Pour the potpourri on the newspaper.

**2.** With your hands, crumble the potpourri into smaller pieces.

**3.** Spread a fabric square flat on your work surface. Scoop about 1/2 cup of the crushed potpourri onto the center of the square.

**4.** Carefully fold up each of the 4 corners of the cloth, and hold them together to form a small bag. The folding will create 4 more corners. Fold these up, too, as shown in the picture.

**5.** Tie a piece of string around the top of the cloth to close up the bag. Tie the string tightly in a double knot.

**6.** Check to make sure there are no gaps in the sachet where the contents could spill out. If there are gaps, tuck these in, wrap the string around a second time, and tie it. Cut off any extra string.

**7.** Tie a piece of ribbon around the sachet to cover the string. Wrap the ribbon around a second time and tie it in a small bow.

**8.** Repeat steps 3 to 7 to make the other three sachets.

# Floral Perfumes

Many colonial women used flower blossoms to make their own perfume, using a process called "enfleurage." They coated two shallow plates with lard, then cut the lard with a knife in a crisscross pattern to absorb more of the blossom scent. Next, they placed flower petals on one plate and fitted the second plate over it with the lard side against the petals. After a few days, they removed the petals and replaced them with fresh ones.

After replacing the petals eight or ten times, the women cut the lard into tiny pieces and placed the pieces in a jar with a little wood alcohol. They aged the mixture for weeks, stirring it daily, then strained it into a clean bottle with some fixative. Most colonial women added their own secret ingredients to create a one-of-a-kind perfume.

# TIME FOR FUN

Sarah had fun drying herbs and making potpourris, but right in the middle of this enjoyable work she had to begin one of the hardest tasks on a colonial farm. It was time to harvest the flax and start the long, difficult job of transforming it into linen cloth.

When colonial families faced a hard task, they made the work lighter and more enjoyable by working together. The Mayhews joined with their neighbors in a flaxing bee, where they prepared the flax for making linen thread. The men cut the flax and carted it into the Mayhews' farmyard. Then everyone joined in to pound the tough fibers on a wooden flaxbrake and clean them with a tool called a swingling knife. Next, they used a wooden plank to separate the long fibers from the short strands. Later in the year, Sarah would spin the long fibers into thread.

Even though the work was hard, the flaxing bee turned into a party. The colonists sang songs and told stories while they worked. Early in the evening, Mrs. Mayhew, Sarah, and the other women served a huge meal. Because the weather was hot and muggy, they made cooling desserts, like berry syllabubs and cranberry ice. They also made Nathan's favorite treat, called blueberry slump. After the meal, while the grown-ups talked, the children played games, including quoits and jackstones.

## PROJECT PLAYING JACKS

The game the colonists called jackstones is known today as jacks. You can buy a set, which includes six 6-pointed metal jacks. Or you can be like colonial children, and use six small stones, pumpkin seeds, or any other small objects that are all the same size. A set will include a small, bouncy ball, but any small ball with a good bounce will do. Or, like colonial children, use a round, smooth stone. (If you use a stone, toss it in the air, rather than try to bounce it.) Here are three of the most popular games.

### MATERIALS

*ball or round, smooth stone*
*6 jacks or other small objects of the same size*
*2 or more players*

### General Rules for Jacks

There are more than 100 different jacks games, but most follow these basic rules:

**1.** Two or more people can play, indoors or out.

**2.** To start a game, a player tosses the ball in the air, scatters the jacks, and catches the ball on one bounce. The player wants the jacks to land pretty close together, but not so close that they're hard to pick up one at a time. Even if he doesn't like the way they landed, he must play the jacks as they lie.

**3.** During play, the player must pick up the jacks and catch the ball on one bounce with the same hand.

**4.** When picking up jacks, the player can touch only the ones he is picking up. If he moves or touches others, his turn is over.

**5.** On any play, each player has only one try. If he makes a mistake, it's the next player's turn.

**6.** If a player makes a mistake and loses his turn, on the next turn he goes back to the beginning of the play in which he made the mistake.

### Game 1: Ones-Through-Sixes
(also called Onesies, Twosies)

*Note: Remember that to start, the first player tosses the ball, scatters the jacks, and catches the ball on one bounce. The ball can bounce only once and a stone must be caught before it lands.*

**1.** To play:

**a.** For ones (onesies): Player 1 tosses the ball again, picks up one jack, then catches the ball on one bounce with the same hand. Player 1 then puts the jack in the other hand and repeats the play, again picking up one jack. Player 1 continues until all six jacks have been picked up, one at a time.

**b.** For twos (twosies): Player 1 bounces the ball, picks up two jacks, catches the ball on one bounce in the same hand, then puts the jacks in the other hand. Player 1 continues until she has picked up all six jacks, two at a time.

**c.** For threes (threesies): Player 1 bounces the ball, picks up three jacks, catches the ball on one bounce

in the same hand. She than puts the jacks in the other hand and repeats the play to pick up the remaining three jacks.

**d.** For fours (foursies): Player 1 picks up 4 jacks on one toss, then two on the next toss.

**e.** For fives (fivesies): Player 1 picks up five jacks at once, then one jack on the next toss.

**f.** For sixes (sixies), Player 1 picks up all six jacks at once and catches the ball on one bounce with the same hand.

**2.** To win: A player who goes from ones through sixes without an error is a winner, but she can be tied if another player also has a perfect round. Remember, when a player loses a turn, she starts the next turn at the beginning of the mistake. If the error was made on threes, for example, the player starts over at the beginning of threes.

### Game 2: Crack the Egg

**1.** To play: Same as Ones-Through-Sixes, but after picking up each jack or jacks, the player must tap them on the playing surface before catching the ball.

**2.** To win: Same as Ones-Through-Sixes.

## Game 3: Sheep Over the Fence

**1.** To play:

**a.** The player stretches one arm on the playing surface, with the arm flat on the surface from the elbow to the hand. This is the fence. Right-handed players use their left arms for the fence; left-handed players use their right arms.

**b.** During play, the player uses the free hand to play and cannot move the fence. The player must pick up each jack or jacks, place (not toss) them over the fence, then catch the ball. After catching the ball, the player transfers the jacks to the hand on her "fence" arm.

**c.** Play proceeds as in Ones-Through-Sixes.

**2.** To win: Same as Ones-Through-Sixes.

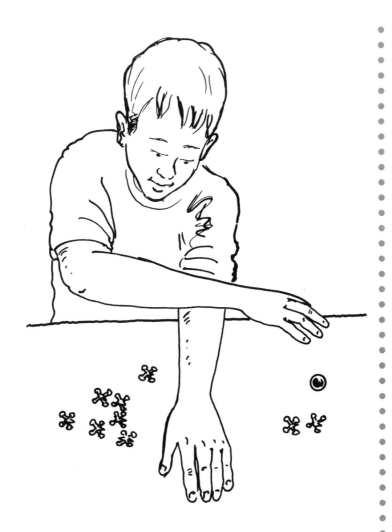

## THE GAME OF QUOITS

Colonial children played quoits with any material that could be shaped into a circle or ring. They often used strips of leather, pieces of rope, or willow branches instead of the heavy iron rings used by wealthier colonists. Quoits are easy to make, the rules of the game are simple, and the contests of skill are exciting. You play the game outdoors with two players, or four players divided into two teams. A flat, grassy area makes the best playing surface.

### MATERIALS

*about 75 inches of rope or clothesline*
*ruler or tape measure*
*scissors*
*masking tape*
*red and black marking pens*
*18- to 20-inch wooden stake or stick*

**1.** To make the game:

**a.** Stretch out the rope and use a ruler or tape measure to measure a 15-inch piece. Cut the rope with the scissors.

**b.** Repeat step a three more times to make four 15-inch pieces of rope. Set the remaining rope aside.

**c.** Loop one 15-inch piece of rope into a circle. Touch the ends together and wrap masking tape around several times where they join. Add more tape if necessary to form a ring that won't fall apart when you toss it.

**d.** Repeat step c with the other three lengths of rope.

**e.** Use the marking pens to color the masking tape on each quoit, making two red and two black.

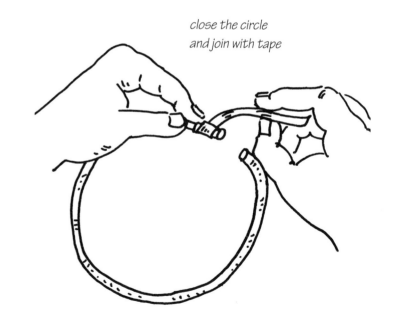

*close the circle
and join with tape*

**f.** Shove the stake or stick firmly into the ground.

**g.** About 20 feet from the stake, lay the remaining piece of rope on the ground so that it is crossways to the stake. This will be your tossing line—the line each player stands behind to toss the quoits.

**h.** Tip the stake a little in the direction of the tossing line.

**i.** Stand at the tossing line and practice tossing the quoits. Move the tossing line forward or back from the stake, or hob, until you have a distance that makes it hard to score a ringer, but not impossible. Once you have settled on the location of the tossing line, players must not step over it when tossing their quoits.

**2.** To play:

**a.** Each player, or team, gets two quoits of the same color, either red or black.

**b.** The first player, or team, tosses their two quoits from behind the tossing line. They aim at the stake, or hob. The second player, or team, follows with two tosses.

**c.** To score:

—When a quoit encircles the hob it's called a ringer. The player or team scores 2 points.

—If a player's quoit is closer to the hob than his opponent's, he scores 1 point. (A quoit leaning against the hob doesn't count extra.)

—If a player throws a ringer and her opponent tops it, neither side scores.

**3.** To win: The first player, or team, to score 21 points wins.

# Quoits and Horseshoes

The game of quoits is more than 2,000 years old. It was played by the ancient Greeks in the original Olympic Games. English settlers brought quoits to the colonies, and it became very popular in the 1700s. The official game was played with iron rings that weighed about three pounds each. Colonial farmers found that iron horseshoes worked just as well, if not better, than the rings. By the early 1800s, the game of horse-shoes became more popular than quoits in both the United States and Canada.

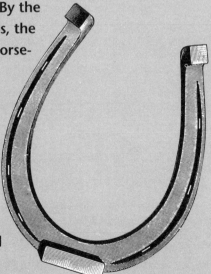

 **BLUEBERRY SLUMP**

Blueberry slump is a strange name for a tasty dessert that's easy to make. No one knows where the name came from, and mystery also surrounds the name of blueberry grunt, a similar dish made with biscuits. You can also make slump with raspberries or blackberries.

### INGREDIENTS
*6 to 8 slices of bread, fresh or stale*
*4 to 5 tablespoons softened butter*
*3 cups blueberries, fresh or frozen*
*½ cup sugar*
*¼ to ½ cup water*
*about 1 cup whipped cream*

### EQUIPMENT
*butter knife*
*medium bowl (should hold 4 cups)*
*saucepan*
*mixing spoon*
*small plate or saucer*
*small pitcher*
*adult helper*

### MAKES
*about 6 servings*

**1.** Break six slices of bread in half and butter them on one side.

**2.** Fit the bread into the bowl, butter side up. The bread should completely cover the bottom and sides of the bowl. If there are open spaces, break another slice of bread and butter it on one side. If necessary, break off smaller buttered pieces and press them into the gaps.

**3.** Place the blueberries, sugar, and water in a saucepan. Mix with the spoon.

**4.** Ask your adult helper to put the saucepan on the stove and bring the mixture to a simmer. Cook gently for about 10 minutes if you're using fresh blueberries; about 5 minutes if using frozen. Stir occasionally with the mixing spoon. Add more water if necessary as the mixture simmers.

**5.** While the berries are cooking, butter one more slice of bread. Do not break this piece in half.

**6.** Have the adult turn off the heat and help you pour the blueberry mixture into the bread-lined bowl.

**7.** Place the whole slice of bread over the top, butter side down. Fold the side pieces over to meet the edges of the top piece.

**8.** Place the small plate or saucer topside down on top of the blueberry and bread mixture. Press down firmly. Lots of juice will flow up to the top.

**9.** Pour off as much of the liquid as you can into the small pitcher. Set aside to serve with the dessert.

**10.** Chill the slump and the extra sauce for 2 to 3 hours. Serve it in small bowls. Pour a little of the extra sauce over each serving and top with a little whipped cream.

 CRANBERRY ICE

During the winter, colonists cut ice from ponds, packed it in straw, and stored it in caves or ice houses. This worked well enough so that they usually had a little ice, even in the summer months.

Ice cream was not invented until the late 1700s, but the colonists enjoyed a variety of cold fruit desserts called "ices." Cranberry ice was a colonial favorite, and you'll find it makes a delicious and healthy substitute for ice cream.

### INGREDIENTS

*2 cups fresh cranberries*
*3½ cups water*
*1½ cups sugar*
*1 teaspoon lemon juice*

### EQUIPMENT

*2- to 3-quart saucepan, with lid*
*mixing spoon*
*large strainer*
*mixing bowl*
*2 metal or plastic ice cube trays with dividers that can be removed, or plastic freezer container*
*fork*
*adult helper*

### MAKES
*about 1 quart*

**1.** Wash the cranberries under cold running water. Throw away any with blemishes.

**2.** Place the cranberries in the saucepan and add the water.

**3.** Have the adult put the covered saucepan on the stove and bring the mixture to a boil.

**4.** As soon as the mixture is boiling, have the adult reduce the heat to low. Simmer for about 10 minutes, stirring the mixture a few times as it cooks. When the cranberries soften and break open, have the adult turn off the heat.

**5.** While the mixture is still warm, have the adult pour it through a strainer into the mixing bowl.

**6.** Press the cranberries against the strainer with the spoon to press as much juice through as you can. Throw away the cranberry skins.

**7.** Add the sugar and lemon juice. Stir well until all the sugar has dissolved.

**8.** Pour the mixture into the ice cube trays (with the dividers removed), and place them in the freezer for about 3 hours. Every 20 or 30 minutes, stir the cranberry ice with a fork. This will break up the solid pieces that form on the bottom and sides.

**9.** Freeze for another 30 minutes without stirring. The finished cranberry ice will look and feel like a smooth sherbet. Serve it like ice cream or sherbert, or mix it with club soda for a slush-like drink.

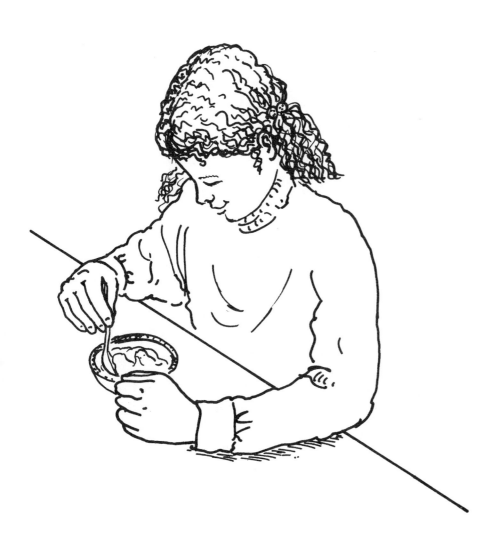

# A Special Syllabub

John Adams (1735–1826) was a colonist who became a leader of the American Revolution, and later the new nation's second president. His favorite syllabub was a hot syllabub drink made with brandy, hard cider, nutmeg, lemon juice, and milk. In order to make the drink foamy, the colonists poured the milk from a height of two feet or more. Another way they made it froth was to milk the cow directly into the pitcher of syllabub!

The first syllabubs were made in England, and English colonists brought the idea to America. These early syllabubs were made with Champagne, and the name *Syllabub* comes from *Sillery*, the Champagne region of France, and *bub*, an English word for a bubbling drink. Syllabubs were especially popular at Christmastime.

 **BERRY SYLLABUB**

Syllabubs were another cooling colonial dessert. Colonists made their own juice from scratch by crushing berries and straining off the juice, but you can make yours from any kind of bottled berry juice. A syllabub is quick and easy to make. Either eat it plain or use it as a topping on angel food cake, yogurt, or ice cream.

## INGREDIENTS
*1 cup unsweetened berry juice, raspberry or strawberry (Grapefruit can also be used.)*
*¼ cup sugar*
*2 cups heavy cream*

## EQUIPMENT
*mixing bowl*
*mixing spoon*
*eggbeater or wire whisk*

## MAKES
*about 3 cups*

**1.** Pour the juice into the mixing bowl.

**2.** Add the sugar, a little at a time, until the juice tastes as sweet as you like it. Keep stirring until the sugar has dissolved completely.

**3.** Pour in the cream. Beat the mixture vigorously with the eggbeater or with the wire whisk until it is thick and stiff enough to form peaks.

**4.** Chill it in the refrigerator for 1 hour. Serve the syllabub in ice cream dishes or as a topping.

# THE ART OF WRITING

Sarah and Nathan missed their Uncle Samuel. The children decided to write letters to him, telling him about the fun of the flaxing bee, and wishing him good fortune on his next voyage.

Writing letters was the only way Sarah and Nathan could keep in touch with Uncle Samuel and their other friends and relatives who lived a long distance away. Like most colonists, Sarah and Nathan took the act of writing very seriously. They formed the letters in their words carefully, trying to achieve the perfect shape, especially for the fancy capital letters. The children wrote with quill pens made of goose feathers. They used ink they made themselves out of berries, walnut shells, and indigo.

After writing her letter, Sarah decided she would start keeping a diary or journal. She used a copybook she had been given for practicing her letters. To make the book special, she asked her mother to show her how to make marbled paper to paste on the inside covers.

 **MARBLED PAPER**

In colonial times, people used paper with marble designs to decorate the inside covers of books, called endpapers. The paper imitated the swirls and patterns found in marble. Marbled paper is still very popular today, not just for endpapers, but for covering boxes and other containers.

For your marbled paper project, choose any two colors you think will work well with a light shade of construction paper. You can buy artist's paint and thinner in the art supply section of discount department stores, or at hobby, craft, and art supply stores. Once you've discovered the fun of marbling, you can make marbled paper to cover pencil holders, lunch boxes, and other items. The marbling never comes out the same way twice.

## MATERIALS
*several sheets of newspaper*
*any pan large enough to hold a sheet of construction*
    *paper flat*
*tap water*
*2 small paper cups*
*small bottles or tubes of artist's oil paint: any 2 colors*
*small bottle of paint thinner or mineral spirits*
*craft stick*
*small paintbrush*
*1 sheet of 8-by-10-inch construction paper: any color*
    *in a light shade*

*2 to 3 paper towels*
*ruler*
*pencil*
*scissors*
*small spiral-bound notebook, about 5 x 7 inches*
*white glue*

**1.** Spread several sheets of newspaper on your work surface.

**2.** Fill the pan with 2 to 3 inches of lukewarm water. Set the pan on the newspaper.

**3.** Pour a small amount of each different-colored oil paint into separate paper cups.

**4.** Add a few drops of paint thinner to each cup. Mix with a craft stick..

**5.** Dip the paintbrush into one color and load up the brush with as much paint as it will hold.

**6.** Hold the brush over the pan. Allow the paint to drip from the brush into the water, sprinkling the drops in several different places on the surface of the water. Add more paint to the brush if necessary, until you have 10 to 15 drops on the water.

**7.** Repeat steps 4 and 5 with the second color.

**8.** Use the craft stick to make a slow, swirling motion on the surface of the water and paint. The drops of paint will stretch out into string-like patterns. *Note: Don't stir too much or the paint swirls will run together.*

**9.** Spread out the paper towels next to the pan. Hold the sheet of construction paper by the corners as shown and gently slide it into the water until it lies flat. Lift the paper out and lay it on paper towels to dry, paint side up.

**10.** When the marbled paper is dry, trim it with scissors to fit the front cover, or the inside cover, of the notebook. To do this, use a ruler to measure the cover, then use the pencil to draw light lines of the measurements on the back of the paper. Cut on the lines.

**11.** Spread white glue thinly but evenly on the back of the paper and fix it in place. Use your notebook as is, or repeat the activity to make a second sheet for the outside or inside back cover.

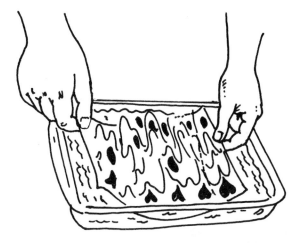

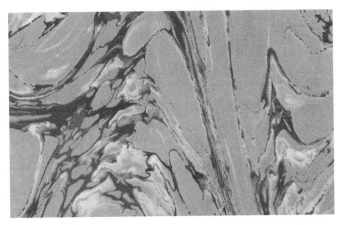

# Postal Problems

There was no real postal service in the 1730s, so mail delivery was not a simple matter for the colonists. The best chance of having a letter reach its destination was to give it to someone who was traveling in the same direction. The traveler would usually drop off the letter at a shop or tavern. Sometimes, the minister would announce the arrival of the letter in church. But there was always the chance that days or weeks would pass before the letter receiver could pick it up. During that time, anyone who saw it lying on a counter felt perfectly free to open it and read the contents!

## PROJECT QUILL PEN

The colonists often made their quill pens from goose feathers. Most farm families raised geese, so goose feathers were plentiful. The colonists also used the feathers of wild turkeys and hawks, but they thought crow feathers were best for making the finest lines.

Don't pick up feathers you find outdoors. You can buy inexpensive feathers in the craft or hobby section of discount department stores or at art supply stores. Look for a feather that is at least 8 inches long. When you're finished, save your quill pen to use with the homemade ink you'll make in the two projects following this one.

### MATERIALS
*large feather, 8 to 12 inches long*
*bowl of warm tap water*
*scissors*
*penknife or craft knife (to be handled only by an adult)*
*cutting board*
*bottle of ink*
*scrap of felt or cotton*
*sheet of paper*
*adult helper*

**1.** Soak the tip of the quill (the hollow, spiny shaft of the feather) in the bowl of warm water for about 15 minutes to soften it..

**2.** If necessary, use scissors to trim off some of the lower feathers so that you have 3 to 4 inches bare at the end of the quill.

**3.** Have the adult use the penknife on the cutting board to cut the tip of the quill in a gentle curve, as shown in the picture. This becomes the nib.

**4.** Have the adult cut a small slit in the center of the nib, which will help control the flow of ink.

**5.** Dip the quill into the ink and blot it gently on the scrap of felt or cotton.

**6.** Practice writing on a sheet of paper by holding the quill at different angles. Re-dip and blot the quill as often as needed. You'll need to experiment a little until writing this way feels comfortable, although don't expect to be very speedy. *Note: When the nib becomes worn or soft, your adult helper can easily cut a new one on the same quill.*

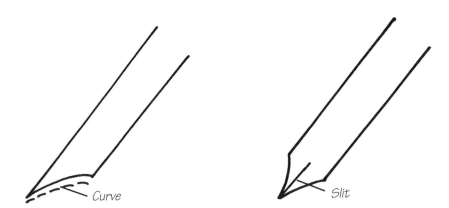

Curve

Slit

 **INDIGO BLUE INK**

The colonists made ink by mixing natural coloring with a little water. They even used the soot that collected on lanterns to make black ink by mixing it with egg yolk and honey. And they used the indigo plant to make blue ink, although they had to follow a complicated process to make it. In this project, you'll follow a simple formula to make blue ink using what's called Prussian blue. It's sold in supermarkets as laundry bluing.

## MATERIALS

*several sheets of newspaper*
*¼ to ½ cup water*
*small jar with lid*
*2 to 4 teaspoons Prussian blue (laundry blueing)*
*craft stick or any similar stir-stick*

**1.** Spread newspaper on your work surface.

**2.** Pour about 1/4 cup water into the jar and set the jar on the newspaper.

**3.** Add 2 teaspoons bluing and stir well until the blueing has dissolved.

**4.** Add more blueing or more water until you have a shade of blue you like. Experiment with your quill pen and adjust the shade of your indigo blue ink, if necessary.

**5.** Use the jar as your inkwell and keep the lid on tight when you're not using the ink. You can store the ink for several weeks.

## PROJECT  BERRY RED INK

The colonists used all kinds of berries to make ink. You may want to experiment with different varieties of berries, especially if you can pick wild berries, like blackberries or raspberries. If you buy berries at a supermarket, however, strawberries will work best. You don't need as many strawberries for a good supply of red ink.

### MATERIALS

*strainer or sieve*

*small bowl*

*½ cup ripe strawberries (Frozen will also work; let them thaw according to the directions on the package.)*

*large spoon*

*½ teaspoon salt*

*½ teaspoon vinegar*

*tap water, if needed*

*small jar with lid*

**1.** Place the strainer over the bowl. Put 2 or 3 strawberries in the strainer.

**2.** With the back of the spoon, mash the strawberries against the bottom of the strainer so the juice drips into the bowl.

**3.** Empty the strainer. (You can save the crushed berries to use as a topping for cereal, yogurt, or ice cream.)

**4.** Place 2 or 3 more berries in the strainer and mash them until the juice drips into the bowl. Continue until you've used up all the berries.

**5.** Add the salt and vinegar to the bowl of juice. Stir well until all the salt has dissolved. If the ink seems too thick, stir in a little water.

# Nature's Paints

To make paint for their houses and furniture, the colonists used natural materials much as they did for fabric dyes and ink. They made black paint by roasting potatoes until they were completely black, then grinding them into powder and adding linseed oil.

The most basic paint was made from buttermilk or sour milk, mixed with lime. To add color, the colonists mixed in plant pigments, just as they did for dyes. They also used pails of earth for reddish or yellowish coloring. They boiled the soil in water, strained it, then pounded it into a powder to add to the buttermilk paint.

The colonists often used whitewash to paint barns, sheds, and fences. A popular New England recipe for glazed whitewash called for cooking rice and sugar in water, then adding skimmed milk and the mineral lime.

When they painted the inside of their houses, colonists got rid of the paint odor by setting out pans of damp hay. The hay absorbed the odors in a day or two.

**6.** Wash out the strainer and place it over the top of the jar. Pour the bowl of berry ink through the strainer into the jar.

**7.** Use the jar as your inkwell. Keep the jar tightly covered and refrigerate it when you're not using it. Berry ink will last about 1 week.

# CHAPTER THREE
# AUTUMN

Like most of their neighbors, the Mayhews produced plenty of food. But they had to plan carefully to make sure their supplies would last through the winter.

The hard work of storing up for the winter began with the autumn harvest. The first frosts could come early in New England, so everyone pitched in to bring the crops in before they could freeze. Nathan and his father harvested the grains. Mrs. Mayhew, Sarah, and the twins picked apples, dug up potatoes and turnips, and hauled in the squashes and pumpkins.

Most of the vegetables and apples were packed in straw and stored in the stonewalled springhouse. The stone walls and the spring water below it kept food cool in warm weather and protected it from freezing in the winter. Autumn was also the time for preserving meat, so Nathan and his father wrapped it in rough cloth and hung it from the rafters of the springhouse.

# THE HARVEST KITCHEN

Sarah and her mother had to fit the harvesting work into their regular daily tasks. On a typical autumn day, Sarah spent part of the morning in the springhouse, bedding apples in straw, then churning butter from that day's milking. Late in the morning, she helped her mother in the kitchen by building a fire in the oven. While the oven heated, they cooked a kettle of fruit in the fireplace to make jam and preserves. In between stirring the simmering fruit, they rolled out and kneaded the dough for bread, then split the dough into loaves.

When the oven was hot, they scooped out the ashes and slid the loaves into the oven on a long wooden paddle called a peel. Mrs. Mayhew then began cutting up meat and vegetables to make a stew for the evening meal, while Sarah built up the fireplace fire and kept a close eye on the baking bread. The delicious smell of the bread and the bubbling fruit gave Sarah and the twins a hearty appetite long before the meal was ready.

## BAKING BREAD

To get an idea of what it was like to prepare even part of a colonial meal, try this project along with the next two—churning butter and making jam. Of course, you won't have to grow the wheat, thresh it (separate the grain from the stalk), and cart it to the village mill to be ground into flour. And you won't have to milk the cows twice a day, or skim the heavy cream off the top, or chop wood for the fireplace and oven! But you will be making food from scratch, just like the colonists did. And when you're finished, you'll have a delicious snack of homemade bread, butter, and jam.

### INGREDIENTS

*2 cups milk*

*1 tablespoon vegetable shortening*

*1½ teaspoons salt*

*½ cup lukewarm tap water*

*1 package or 1 tablespoon active dry yeast*

*2 tablespoons sugar*

*6 cups all-purpose flour*

*4 to 5 tablespoons soft butter*

### EQUIPMENT

*measuring cup*

*small saucepan*

*large mixing bowl*

*large mixing spoon*

*breadboard or countertop*

*waxed paper*

*clean, dry towel*

*table knife*

*rolling pin*

*2 loaf pans*

*2 wire cooling racks*

*adult helper*

### MAKES

*2 loaves*

**1.** Place the milk, shortening, and salt in a small saucepan.

**2.** Ask your adult helper to place the saucepan on the stove and heat it over medium heat. Stir it once or twice with the large mixing spoon.

**3.** When the mixture is hot but not boiling, have the adult remove the pan from the heat. Let the mixture cool to lukewarm.

**4.** Pour the lukewarm tap water into the large mixing bowl. (*Note: The water* must *be lukewarm.*) Sprinkle the yeast into the water and add the sugar. Stir it well, then set it aside for 5 to 10 minutes. (The little bubbles that form are proof that the yeast is working.)

**5.** Add the milk-salt-shortening mixture to the yeast bowl and stir to mix the ingredients.

**6.** Slowly stir in 3 cups of the flour. Beat the mixture with the spoon until it is smooth.

**7.** Begin adding more flour a little at a time. As the dough thickens, mix it with your hands. Add just enough flour so the dough doesn't stick to the sides of the bowl. When finished mixing, you should have at least ½ cup of flour left over.

**8.** Sprinkle some of the leftover flour onto your ball of dough and onto the breadboard (or countertop). Put the dough on the board and let it rest for 5 minutes.

**9.** Knead the dough steadily for about 10 minutes. Push it forward with the heel of your hand, then roll the dough into a ball, push it again, and work the dough with your fingers, like a cat kneading its claws. You'll feel the dough become smooth and elastic. Press two fingers into the dough; if the dough springs back quickly, it's ready.

**10.** Use about 1 tablespoon of soft butter on a piece of waxed paper to grease the mixing bowl.

**11.** Place the dough in the bowl, and cover it with a towel. Let it rise in a warm place for 1 to 1½ hours until it doubles in size. Press two fingers into the dough; if it does not spring back, it's ready.

**12.** Punch the dough down in the center with your fist to let some of the air out. Put it on the bread board and knead it vigorously for 6 to 8 minutes. You can pound it, slam it, and punch it as you knead—in other words, really work the dough.

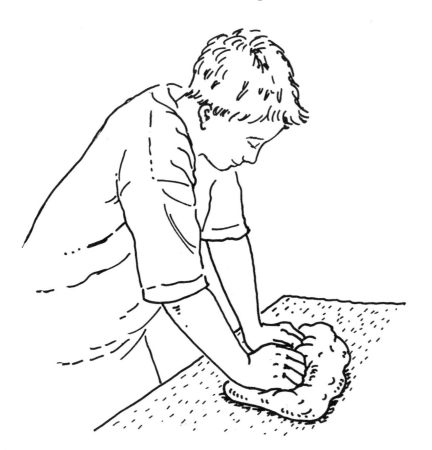

**13.** Cut the dough in half with a table knife. Use the rolling pin to roll out each half into a rectangle. Form each rectangle into a loaf shape with your hands. The loaf should be like the shape of the bread pan.

**14.** Use some of the soft butter to grease the loaf pans, spreading the butter evenly with a piece of waxed paper.

**15.** Place the loaves in the pans, seam side down, and spread the last of the butter on the top of each loaf. Cover the loaves with the towel and let them rise again for about 1 hour.

**16.** While the loaves are rising, have the adult preheat the oven to 425°F.

**17.** When the loaves are ready, have the adult place the pans on the lower shelf of the oven, not touching each other or the sides of the oven. Bake for 10 minutes, then lower the heat to 350°F. Bake for another 20 to 25 minutes, until the crusts are golden brown.

**18.** Have the adult remove the pans from the oven and gently knock the loaves onto the wire racks to cool. The bread is still baking, so don't slice it until it has cooled for about 45 minutes.

# Bread Variety

The colonists baked many different kinds of bread, often using oats, rye, barley, or corn instead of wheat for flour. During the autumn harvest, they often made special harvest loaves by combining three or four different grains. They also made bread from pumpkin, squash, and cranberries. These were called quick breads—the batter contained no yeast so they didn't have to wait for the dough to rise.

Colonists made yeast by mixing mashed potatoes, sugar, salt, and warm water in a small pottery jug and letting it age for a few days. One cup of this mixture produced enough yeast for two loaves of bread.

People in the 1700s did not know that yeast is made up of microscopic single-cell fungi. These tiny fungi feed off the sugar, producing carbon dioxide that makes the dough rise. The colonists knew only that the yeast was working if it produced small bubbles. If no bubbles appeared, they had to make fresh yeast.

# PROJECT CHURNING BUTTER

The colonists made butter in wooden or pottery churns, using the thick cream that rose to the top of the milk. The churns had wooden paddles built into the lid, and the cream was stirred, or churned, until it turned into butter. Because several pounds of butter were made at a time, the churning required a good deal of muscle power. You'll be making only a small amount of butter, so you can do it without a churn. It won't take much time for the cream to change into butter.

## INGREDIENTS
1½ cups heavy cream (whipping cream)
pinch of salt

## EQUIPMENT
1-quart jar with lid (A canning jar is perfect, but any sturdy jar with a tight-fitting lid will do.)
5 or 6 clean marbles or small, well-washed stones
tap water
mixing spoon
rubber spatula
small dish
butter mold (optional)

## MAKES
about 3/4 cup

**1.** Let the cream stand in a warm place until it reaches room temperature.

**2.** Pour the cream into the jar. Add the marbles or stones and tighten the lid.

**3.** Shake the jar steadily up and down, and from side to side. Keep shaking vigorously until globs of butter form in the jar. The butter will begin to form within 5 minutes.

**4.** When the butter globs have stopped forming, open the jar and pour off the liquid, which is called buttermilk. Remove the marbles.

**5.** Rinse the butter in cool, running water. Pour out the water gently so the butter remains in the jar.

**6.** Add a pinch of salt to the butter. Stir it well with the mixing spoon to blend the ingredients.

**7.** Use the spatula to scrape the butter into a small dish. If you have a butter mold, press the butter into it, or use the spatula and your fingers to form it into a square or rectangle.

**8.** Chill the butter in the refrigerator for 20 to 30 minutes before serving.

# Printing Butter

The colonists liked to decorate just about everything they made, even butter. Instead of serving the butter plain, they used wooden butter molds made out of pine or poplar. They carved designs into the molds, like birds, flowers, or stalks of wheat. When they pressed the butter into the mold, they created what was called print butter.

When colonists bought butter on market day, they looked for the print of the family known for the tastiest butter. One farm wife had her husband carve some advertising into her butter mold. It said, "Good butter. Taste it."

# MAKING JAM

In this project, you'll make ready-to-use jam that can be stored in the refrigerator for a few days. If you want to make a larger amount and store it for a longer period, you'll have to use special canning jars. You can find instructions for canning in many cookbooks.

## INGREDIENTS

*1 pint fresh fruit (Strawberries or peaches work well.)*
*½ cup sugar*
*¼ to ½ cup water*

## EQUIPMENT

*colander or strainer*
*paring knife (to be handled only by an adult)*
*cutting board*
*1-quart saucepan with lid*
*mixing spoon*
*candy thermometer*
*1-quart bowl*
*rubber spatula*
*adult helper*

## MAKES

*about ¾ pint, or 8 to 10 servings*

**1.** Wash the fruit well and drain it in the colander or strainer.

**2.** Ask the adult to remove the hulls or pits from the fruit with a paring knife and then cut the fruit into thin slices on the cutting board.

**3.** Sprinkle ¼ cup of the sugar on the bottom of the saucepan. Add half of the sliced fruit, then sprinkle 2 tablespoons of sugar on top. Add the rest of the fruit and then the rest of the sugar.

**4.** Allow the fruit and sugar mixture to stand at least 4 to 5 hours or overnight.

**5.** When the mixture is ready, add the water to the saucepan and stir to mix the ingredients.

**6.** Ask the adult to place the covered saucepan on the stove and heat the mixture over medium-high heat until it boils.

**7.** As soon as the fruit mixture starts to boil, have the adult reduce the heat to a simmer. Keep the saucepan covered and simmer for about 30 minutes. Stir the jam frequently, and add more water if it becomes too thick.

**8.** After about 30 minutes of cooking, have the adult help you check the temperature with a candy thermometer. Continue to simmer the jam until it reaches 230°F. At this temperature, the jam is ready.

**9.** Have the adult turn off the heat and pour the jam into a bowl. Use the spatula to scrape the sides of the pan well to get all the jam.

**10.** Allow the jam to cool for an hour or two before you serve it. Remember: Ready-to-use jam can be stored in the refrigerator for only a few days.

# NATIVE AMERICAN NEIGHBORS

Late in the harvest season, the Mayhews took a day off from farm work to visit a nearby Indian village. The villagers were Mohegans, one of the Algonquin tribes scattered throughout New England. The Mohegans had always been friendly with the colonists, unlike some of the other Algonquin tribes.

Mr. Mayhew often traded with the Mohegans, and this time he took the family along while he exchanged some smoked meat for Mohegan deerskins. Sarah and Nathan were thrilled to see the Mohegan village with its trim farm fields. They watched a harvest ceremony and made friends with a girl named Moo'quin, which means "fawn." Moo'quin sat with them during a feast of clam chowder and roasted corn. The children were delighted when they heard their parents invite Moo'quin and her family to the Mayhew farm for a

cornhusking bee planned for the following week.

After the meal, Moo'quin showed Sarah how to make a Mohegan headband. Then she showed Nathan how the Algonquin tribes made their drums and drumsticks.

# PROJECT ALGONQUIN DRUM

Native Americans made their drums by stretching wet deerskin, called rawhide, over the drum base. As the rawhide dried, it shrunk a little, making the drumhead tight and producing a sound that could be heard over great distances. Instead of rawhide, you'll make your drumhead out of wrapping paper and cheesecloth. Two coats of acrylic varnish will help strengthen the drumhead and improve the sound. While your drum won't be quite the same as rawhide, you'll be surprised by how well it works.

*Note: Acrylic varnish is not oil-based or toxic, so it can be used safely. Spray cans, however, are not recommended.*

## MATERIALS

*several sheets of newspaper*
*large fruit juice can or round oatmeal container*
*heavy brown wrapping paper, about 10 inches square*
   *(A shopping bag works well.)*
*pencil*
*ruler*
*scissors*
*10-inch-square piece of cheesecloth, or any thin cloth*
*thick rubber band or about 24 inches of string*
*acrylic varnish (available wherever paints are sold)*
*2 paintbrushes, each about 1 inch wide*
*poster paint: 1 color of your choice*
*red and black marking pens*

**1.** Spread several sheets of newspaper over your work area.

**2.** Place the can or container on the sheet of brown wrapping paper. With the pencil, trace around the container on the paper.

**3.** Draw a second circle freehand about 2 inches larger around the first circle. Cut out the larger circle with scissors.

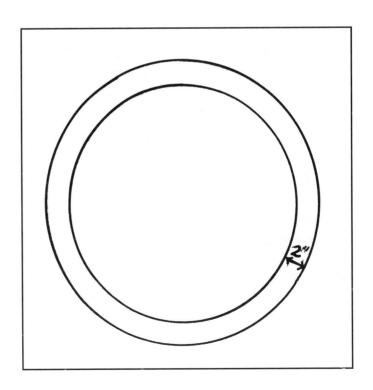

**4.** Position the wrapping paper circle on a piece of cheesecloth. Cut a cheesecloth circle the same size as the paper circle.

**5.** Position the wrapping paper circle over the open end of the oatmeal container or can. Line up the first circle you drew on the paper with the top of the container.

**6.** Fold down the 2-inch paper border around the outside edge of the container. Make folds in the paper where necessary so that it fits snugly over the top of the container and the sides.

**7.** Place the cheesecloth circle on top of the paper and fold down the edges in the same way. Fasten the cheesecloth-paper drumhead in place with a thick rubber band or tie it tightly with string. (To tie the string, wrap it around the container twice, then tie a firm double knot.)

**8.** Use one of the paintbrushes to cover the cheesecloth and paper drumhead with two coats of acrylic varnish. Allow the varnish to dry completely between coats: 1 to 2 hours.

**9.** Use the second paintbrush to apply one or two coats of poster paint, any color, to the sides of the drum. Don't paint the drumhead.

**10.** Copy the design for the drumhead shown here lightly in pencil on the cheesecloth. Go over the design with red and black marking pens, using any combination of the colors you wish.

**11.** Your Algonquin drum is now ready. Play it with the drumstick you'll make in the next activity, or just use your fingers and hands.

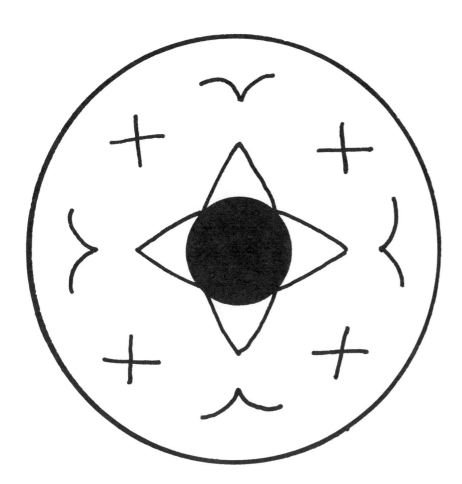

# Hard Choices for Native Americans

As the colonies grew during the 1600s and the 1700s, the Native American peoples found themselves being crowded out by the colonists. Some tribes, like the Cherokee in the South and the Mohegans in New England, hoped to live in peace with the Europeans. They became Christians and adopted the colonists' methods of farming.

Other tribes decided to fight for their lands. In New England, the Pequot and Wampanoag tribes were nearly destroyed in wars against the colonists. During the American Revolution (1775–1783), the Mohawks and other tribes of the Iroquois Confederation fought on the English side against the Americans. They hoped that the English would help them keep their tribal lands. Still other tribes moved farther west or into Canada where they joined other tribes. As Americans pushed westward, the conflict over the land continued until the late 1800s.

# ALGONQUIN DRUMSTICK

The woodland tribes of the Northeast made many kinds of drumsticks, some for different drums, some to produce different sounds from the same drum. They used either a curved drumstick, made from a thin piece of hardwood bent into a circle, or a straight drumstick, usually with padding but sometimes without. In this project, you'll make a straight, padded woodland drumstick.

## MATERIALS

*white glue*
*12-inch-long stick, chopstick, or dowel*
*3 or 4 strips of rag, about 1/2 inch wide and*
  *4 inches long*
*4½-inch square of cotton cloth, any solid color*
*12-inch-long piece of string or a strong rubber band*
*marking pens: red, black, and yellow (or blue)*

**1.** Spread a few drops of glue to cover about two inches of one end of the stick.

**2.** To pad the drumstick, wrap one of the rag strips around the glued end. Add a few drops of glue to the end of the rag to hold it in place.

**3.** Add 2 or 3 additional rag strips on top of the first and glue them in place.

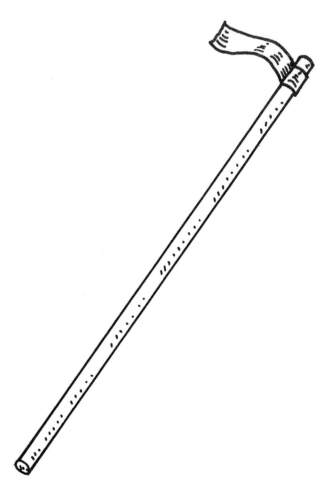

**4.** Place the square piece of cloth over the end of the drumstick. Fold it down over the padding. Tie it firmly in place by winding the string around it several times, then tie the string in a double knot. (Or wind the rubber band around the padding several times until it holds the rags firmly.)

**5.** Use marking pens to make different colored bands around the handle of the drumstick. Make the bands wide or narrow, and use any combination of the colors you wish. Now test your drumstick on your Algonquin drum.

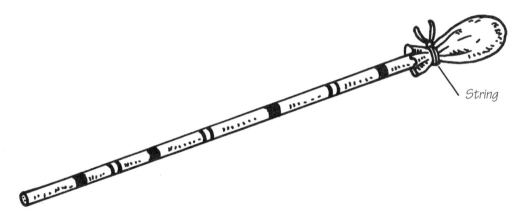

String

## Native American Drums

Drums were important in the life of all Native American tribes. They used some drums to call the members of the tribe together, others as part of healing ceremonies, and still others for religious ceremonies, storytelling, or social events. The drums ranged in size from small circles of wood no more than three inches high to large, hollowed-out logs. They sometimes filled the log drums part way with water to produce a deeper sound that could be heard over great distances.

# PROJECT NATIVE AMERICAN HEADBAND

When the weather was cold, the people of the Algonquin tribes wore hats of soft deerskin, decorated with feathers. They called these *gus-to-weh*, which means "real hat." The rest of the year, both boys and girls wore a simple headband decorated with painted symbols or beads and sometimes a feather.

You can make a similar headband, using felt instead of deerskin. A plain headband, decorated with colorful squares, looks great. You can also glue on small beads or sequins, or add a feather. You can find beads, sequins, and feathers in the craft section of discount department stores, as well as at craft and hobby stores.

## MATERIALS
*several sheets of newspaper*
*1½-by-18-inch strip of felt: tan, brown, or any*
  *light shade*
*ruler*
*one-hole paper punch*
*white glue or craft glue*
*two 10-inch-long rawhide laces (sold as shoelaces)*
  *(String or twine will also work.)*
*scissors*
*six 1-inch-square scraps of felt in any bright colors*
*12 to 18 small beads, any colors (optional)*
*sequins (optional)*
*feather (optional)*

**1.** Spread the newspaper over your work area.

**2.** Lay the felt strip flat on your work surface. Use the hole punch to make two holes about ¼ inch in from each end. You should have a total of four holes, two at each end, as shown in the picture.

**3.** Fold over each end about 1 inch. Punch through each of the four holes you made so that the hole punch goes through the layer of fabric underneath.

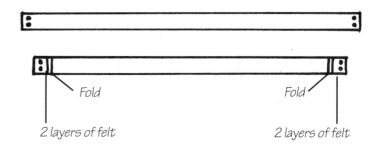

Fold          Fold

2 layers of felt          2 layers of felt

**4.** Unfold the ends, then glue them back together, making sure the holes are lined up. (Spread the glue evenly and thinly. If it's too thick, the glue will show through the fabric.) Allow the glue to dry.

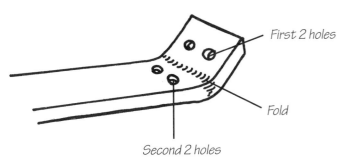

First 2 holes

Fold

Second 2 holes

**5.** Turn the felt strip over, so that the folds are underneath. Run a rawhide lace (or piece of string) through both holes in one end of the strip. Tie a double knot about 2 inches beyond the end of the headband.

**6.** Cut off one loose end of the rawhide, but leave the other for tying the headband on your head.

**7.** Repeat steps 5 and 6 with the other rawhide lace (or string) on the other end of the headband.

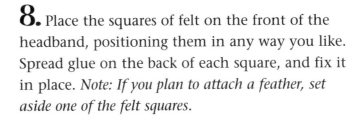

**8.** Place the squares of felt on the front of the headband, positioning them in any way you like. Spread glue on the back of each square, and fix it in place. *Note: If you plan to attach a feather, set aside one of the felt squares.*

**9.** [optional] Glue on small beads or sequins in any pattern you wish.

**10.** [optional] To add a feather, place a patch of felt over the quill end of the feather. Glue the patch to the back part of the headband near the laces. The feather can be straight up and down, or tipped at an angle.

**11.** To wear the headband, tie the rawhide lace or string at the back of your head with a single knot, then a bow, as if you were tying a shoe.

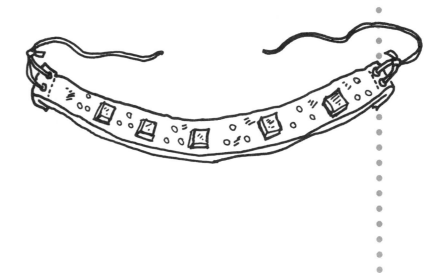

# HARVEST FROLICS

On the day of the Mayhews' cornhusking bee, Moo'quin and her family arrived early in the morning, and a dozen village families arrived soon after. Everyone was in a holiday spirit. Cornhusking was more of a celebration than a hard work session, so the Mayhews and the other colonists often called it a frolic. They were celebrating the fact that husking the corn was the last major task of the harvest season. Even though husking took a lot of time, it was so easy that it seemed like a party.

The ears of corn were piled in a great heap on the floor of the barn. Men, women, and children gathered around the pile and everyone tore off the husks as fast as they could. Some of the boys made a contest out of it to see who could husk the most ears in the shortest time.

When the husking was finished, the women helped Sarah and Mrs. Mayhew serve a big meal. Then, with a full moon lighting the farmyard, the grown-ups talked while the children played games like blindman's buff and had bubble-blowing contests. Moo'quin showed Sarah and her friends how to play a game called stick toss, and how to make dolls quickly and easily out of corncobs.

# PROJECT CORNCOB DOLL

The dolls young children played with in the 1700s were usually very simple. Some dolls were only round sticks with faces painted on them. More elaborate dolls were made with scraps of cloth and stuffed with rags or cornsilk. The people of the Eastern Native American tribes also formed simple dolls out of corncobs. Sometimes they made delicate deerskin clothing decorated with beads for these dolls. But most of the time, they simply attached pieces of cloth and painted a face, much as you'll be doing in this project.

## MATERIALS

*several sheets of newspaper*
*1 corncob with the corn kernels removed*
*ruler*
*table knife*
*pencil*
*two 3-by-8-inch scraps of felt or cotton, in any light color*
*scissors*
*red and black marking pens*
*white glue or craft glue*
*16-inch piece of lightweight yarn: brown or black*
*6-inch piece of narrow ribbon, any color*

**1.** Spread the newspaper over your work surface.

**2.** Break the corncob at both the narrow end and the stem end. You want a cob about 6 inches long that will stand upright. Use the table knife to scrape the cob so that the surface is fairly even.

**3.** Copy the top pattern on page 76 for the doll's top in pencil on one strip of cloth. Copy the pattern below it for the skirt on the other strip of fabric. Cut out the top and skirt.

**4.** Wrap each strip of cloth completely around the corncob. The ends of each strip should overlap about ½ inch. Trim off any extra material.

**5.** With red and black marking pens, add a design to the two pieces of fabric. Either use the design shown in the drawing on page 76, or create your own.

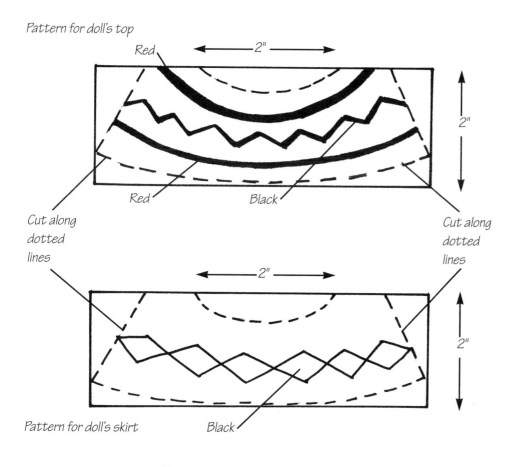

*Pattern for doll's top*

Red

2"

2"

Red          Black

Cut along
dotted
lines

Cut along
dotted
lines

2"

2"

*Pattern for doll's skirt*          Black

**6.** Wrap the skirt around the base of the corn-cob. Glue the fabric to itself at the ½-inch overlap.

**7.** Wrap the top around the corncob above the skirt, leaving about 2 inches of corncob above the top. Glue as in step 6.

**8.** With the black marking pen, draw the eyes, nose, and mouth on the doll as shown in the picture.

**9.** Cut the yarn into eight 2-inch lengths. Glue 4 yarn strips to each side of the doll's head so that the strands fall on either side of the face.

**10.** Wrap the narrow ribbon around the doll's head. The ends of the ribbon should overlap about ½ inch. Trim off any extra ribbon.

**11.** Glue the ribbon to itself at the ½-inch overlap to form a headband. Your corncob doll is finished.

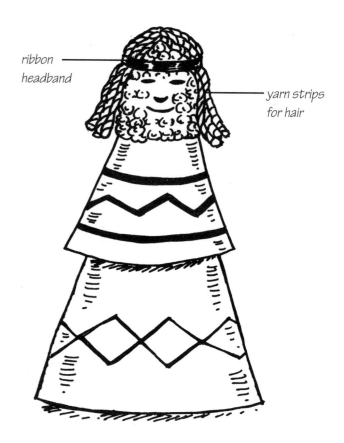

ribbon
headband

yarn strips
for hair

## PROJECT — BLINDMAN'S BUFF

Called "blindman's buff," this game was popular with adults as well as children in the 1700s. In earlier times, the players not only spun the blindfolded person around, but shoved or buffeted him or her, which is how the name "buff" started. The colonists played the game according to the rules used here. Any number can play; the more the better.

### MATERIALS
*handful of sticks or straws of different lengths*
*scarf or similar cloth for the blindfold*
*5 or more players*

**1.** To start: Players draw sticks or straws to see who will be the first blindfolded player. The player who draws the shortest one wears the blindfold.

**2.** To play:
a. One player ties a blindfold securely around the person who is "it." The other players form a circle around her.
b. One or two players step forward. They spin the blindfolded player around two or three times, then rejoin the circle.
c. The players join hands and walk in a circle around the blindfolded player. The player who is "it" claps three times and the circle stops.
d. "It" points at one player who must step into the circle. The blindfolded player has one chance to guess who the person is. If the guess is right, that person takes the blindfold. If the guess is wrong (and it usually is), the blindfolded player tries to catch the player by touching him on the head, clothing, or feet.

## Game Variations

Colonists who came to America from other countries often played the same games, but with different names and often with different rules. Swedish colonists who settled in New Jersey and Delaware played blindman's buff, but they called it *blindbock*, which means "blind buck." German settlers in Pennsylvania called the game *Blinderkuh*, meaning "blind cow." And to French settlers in the Hudson River Valley of New York colony, the game was known as *colin-maillard*. This name came from a legend about a heroic knight who was temporarily blinded in battle but continued to swing his sword at the charging enemy. Over the years, many people forgot the meaning of the word "buff" and began calling the game "blindman's bluff."

**e.** The blindfolded player then has one more chance to guess who the player is. If the guess is right, they change places and the player becomes "it." If the guess is wrong, the player rejoins the circle, the blindfolded player is spun around again, and the game continues.

 **BUBBLE BLOWERS**

Since ancient times, children and adults have been fascinated by blowing soap bubbles. For colonial children, the best time for bubble blowing was on wash day when a large kettle of suds steamed in the farmyard. By the early 1700s, colonists were coming up with all sorts of devices for making bubbles, and this project lets you try several methods.

To make bubbles that last longer, add a few drops of glycerin to your soap mixture. You can buy a small bottle of glycerin at drugstores and most supermarkets.

Bubble blowing can be messy, so always use your bubble blowers outdoors. Try a contest with a friend to see who can make the biggest and longest lasting bubbles.

### MATERIALS
*scissors*
*3 drinking straws*
*12-inch-long lightweight, flexible wire*
*¾ cup tap water*
*small bowl*
*¼ cup liquid dishwashing detergent*
*1 tablespoon glycerin (optional)*

**1.** Use the scissors to cut one drinking straw at an angle, as shown in the drawing.

**2.** Use the scissors to cut 3 or 4 slits about ½ inch long in the second straw. Bend back the sections that have been cut, as shown.

**3.** Cut the third straw your own way. You could either cut it at a steeper angle, or with 2 slits instead of 3 or 4.

**4.** Bend one end of the wire into a circle. Wind the end around the stem, as shown in the drawing.

**5.** Twist the other end of the wire to make a small handle.

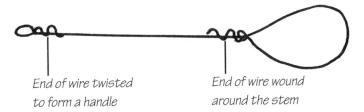

End of wire twisted to form a handle

End of wire wound around the stem

**6.** Pour the water into the small bowl. Add the liquid detergent. Optional: Add the glycerin.

**7.** Stir the mixture gently with one of the straws—you don't have to create suds.

**8.** Dip the cut end of one of the straws into the mixture and blow gently through the other end. Repeat with the other two straws. Each of the cut straws will make bubbles of different shapes and sizes.

**9.** Use the wire blower by dipping the circle into the soap solution so that a soapy film covers the circle. Hold the wire by the handle and blow gently against the film, or wave the wire like a wand to make multiple small bubbles.

# NATIVE AMERICAN STICK TOSS GAME

PROJECT

Almost every Native American tribe in North America played some form of stick toss. They made the sticks from the rib bones of deer, and painted designs on them with paints made from clay and berries. You can make the game with craft sticks and marking or felt-tip pens. Work with a partner to make the four game pieces, then see who has the best luck playing stick toss.

## MATERIALS

*4 craft sticks or tongue depressors*
*fine-tip red, yellow, and black marking pens or*
*felt-tip pens*
*15 counting sticks, such as twigs or pencils*
*2, 3, or 4 players*

**1.** To make the game: Use the marking pens or felt-tip pens to color the four craft sticks as shown in the drawing. *Note: Only the rain stick has markings on the back. The lightning, sun, and four directions sticks are blank on the back sides.*

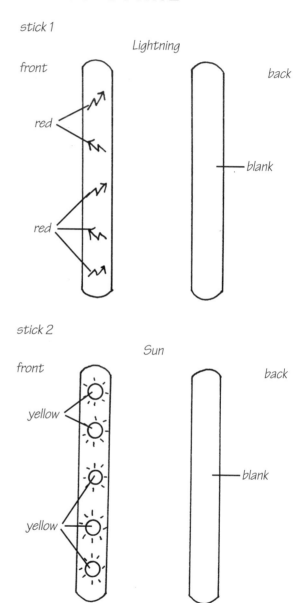

stick 1

Lightning

front

red

red

back

blank

stick 2

Sun

front

yellow

yellow

back

blank

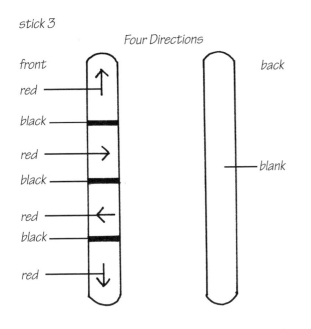

stick 3

Four Directions

front · red · black · red · black · red · black · red

back · blank

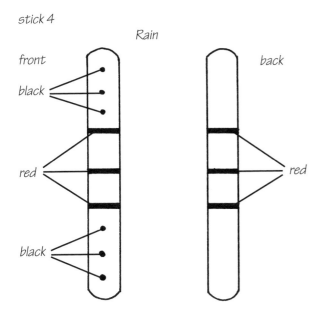

stick 4

Rain

front · black · red · black

back · red

**2.** To play:

**a.** The players sit facing one other. (If four people play, form teams of two.) Place the 15 counting sticks off to one side.

**b.** The first player picks up the four craft sticks. Using just the fingertips of one hand, she holds the sticks in a bunch by their tops, then gently tosses them in the air so that they land on the playing surface between the players.

**c.** The player who tossed the sticks scores points according to which sides of the sticks are facing up. The scoring is as follows:

> Front side of four directions: 4 points
>
> Front side of rain: 3 points
>
> Front side of lightning: 1 point
>
> Front side of sun: 1 point
>
> Back side of lightning, sun, or four directions: 0 points each
>
> Back side of rain: cancels out the entire score for that toss

**d.** After the player tosses, she picks up the number of counting sticks equal to her score. For example, if her toss was rain, lightning, blank, blank, her score would be 4 points. She would then take 4 counting sticks from the pile. If she tossed the back side of rain, however, her score would be canceled and her turn would be over.

# A Love of Games

Games were popular in all Native American tribes, and each tribe had its favorites. There were two main types of games. There were games of chance, similar to modern games with dice or playing cards. The other type of games required athletic skill. Many of these games involved throwing darts or spears, often at a moving target. All sorts of ball games were played; in fact, the modern game of lacrosse was invented by Native Americans.

**e.** As long as player 1 continues to score, she keeps tossing. As soon as she tosses the back side of rain, it is the next player's turn.

**f.** When all 15 counting sticks have been removed from the pile, the player scoring points takes the correct number of counting sticks from the other player's or team's pile.

**3.** To win: The game officially ends when one player has gotten all 15 counting sticks. But it seldom works that way. The game can continue for a long time, so the players usually decide when the game ends. In that case, the player with the most counting sticks wins.

# CHAPTER FOUR

# WINTER

With the coming of winter, life in the Mayhew household changed. School began again for Nathan. When he wasn't in school, he fed the farm animals, cleaned the stalls, chopped firewood, and helped with repairs. Mr. Mayhew's days were different, too. He was helping to build a meeting house in the village.

For Sarah and her mother, daily life did not change as much. They still spent a good part of each day preparing meals. But now that the harvest was in, there was more time to catch up on spinning, weaving, and sewing. Sarah enjoyed working by the warmth of the fireplace while tending to little Benjamin and Anne.

Over evening supper, the family often talked about their plans for the coming year. They were excited about the news in the village that the young schoolmaster was going to accept girls as students. Mrs. Mayhew said the house would seem terribly quiet when Sarah and the twins joined Nathan in the schoolhouse.

# PREPARING FOR WINTER

One of the early winter tasks the children liked best was dipping candles, especially bayberry or beeswax candles. Both gave a good light, burned cleanly, and added a pleasant aroma to the house. But bayberry and beeswax were scarce. It took nearly a bushel of the little white bayberries to make a single pair of candles. The Mayhews didn't make them often, and they saved the candles for special occasions.

Most of the time, the family made their candles from tallow. Tallow was nothing more than hard animal fat that had to simmer in a big fireplace kettle for several days before it was ready. The tallow candles tended to smoke and sputter, and mice often found they made a tasty snack. But, when the sun went down, even a tallow candle made a welcome pool of light, the only light the family had at night except for the fireplace.

Mr. Mayhew also showed the children how to make their own candlesticks using clay they had found near the river. And with winter storms on the way, he showed Nathan and Sarah how to look for approaching storms by reading nature's clues.

## PROJECT STORM WATCH

A few colonists had barometers, tools that helped them tell when storms were coming by measuring changes in air pressure. A falling barometer almost always means the weather will grow worse. But most colonial families relied on observation. They watched the sky or the behavior of animals, and they knew what to look for. They weren't always right, but they knew it was better to be prepared for a storm than to be surprised by one. You can try the same techniques, looking for the clues the colonists used. And you don't have to wait for winter. The clues are the same throughout the year.

## MATERIALS

*pencil*
*small notebook or pad*
*directional compass (optional)*
*adult helper*

1. Copy the list of weather signs into your notebook.

### Storm Warning Signs

1. "Red in the morning, sailor take warning."

2. There is a halo or a hazy circle around the moon.

3. Your hair feels limp and doesn't seem to have its usual bounce.

4. Smoke from chimneys or smokestacks hovers in the air or drifts toward the ground.

5. Objects far away look closer than usual.

6. Geese or ducks fly close to the ground.

7. Cows in pasture are lying low.

8. The wind is coming from the east or northeast (especially in eastern United States and Canada).

9. Clouds look very low in the sky.

10. You can smell ground odors from swamps or drainage ditches.

11. Birds and insects are not as active as usual.

## A Storm Watch Poem

One colonist, Dr. Andrew Jenner, wrote his weather clues in a long poem. Here are a few of his lines:

The hollow wind begins to blow,
The clouds look black, the grass
  is low;
The soot falls down, the spaniels
  sleep,
And spiders from their cobwebs
  peep.
Loud quack the ducks, the peacocks
  cry;
The distant hills are looking nigh.

(Reprinted from The New England Farmer's Almanac for 1829, Boston, by Thomas G. Fessenden, titled "Signs of Rain.")

**2.** First thing in the morning, look at the eastern sky (where the sun is shining) as the sun is coming up. If the sky to the east has a red or pinkish glow, it's a good day for a storm watch. You may know the saying, "Red in the morning, sailor take warning." A red morning sky doesn't always mean a storm is coming, however, so you'll need to look for other storm signs, too.

**3.** Take a weather walk with your adult helper, taking your list of weather signs with you.

**4.** When you see a sign on your list, put a check mark next to it.

**5.** On some days you won't find any clues. But on a day when you can check off at least three storm signs, you can predict that bad weather is coming.

**6.** Wait 24 to 48 hours to see if your prediction was correct. Record the type of weather that occurred in your notebook.

**7.** Turn to a new page in your notebook and repeat this activity every few days for several weeks. As you become more skilled at reading the signs, your storm predictions will become more accurate. Remember, though, that even the U.S. Weather Service, with all the latest scientific equipment, cannot always make perfect predictions.

# PROJECT DIPPING CANDLES

For your candle dipping, you'll use paraffin wax, a product that was developed around 1870 to replace tallow. You'll also need an adult helper to work with you.

Follow this procedure to make one pair of candles. To make more candles, use two pounds of wax and a 22-inch piece of candle wicking for each additional pair. After you've made your candles, have an adult light them, then try an evening of only candlelight to give you an idea of nighttime light in colonial days.

## MATERIALS

*a broomstick or any similar pole*
*2 kitchen chairs with backs that are level at the top*
*several sheets of newspaper*
*2 pounds of paraffin wax (available at supermarkets)*
*1 dipping can (An empty and clean 48-ounce fruit juice can works well.)*
*3- or 4-quart ½ full pot of tap water*
*candy thermometer*
*4 tablespoons stearin (optional), available at craft and hobby stores*
*22-inch piece of candle wicking (available at craft and hobby stores) or butcher's string*
*long-handled spoon or piece of doweling*
*ruler*
*clock or timer*
*scissors*
*paring knife (to be handled only by an adult)*
*adult helper*

**1.** Make a hardening rack for your candles by placing a broom or similar pole across the backs of two chairs. Place several sheets of newspaper on the floor beneath the rack to catch drips.

**2.** Place the wax in the dipping can and set it in the pot of water. Ask the adult to bring the water to a simmer, but not a boil. When the wax has melted, have the adult use the candy thermometer to keep the wax at a temperature between 150°F and 170°F.
*Caution: Don't let the wax get too hot. If it begins to smoke, have the adult turn off the heat until it has cooled down. Be careful not to drip wax on the stove burner.*

**3.** [optional] Add 12 tablespoons of stearin to the melted wax. This is not essential, but it helps the wax to harden.

**4.** When the wax is between 150°F and 170°F, fold the 22-inch piece of candle wicking in half. Place the wick at the fold over the middle of the long-handled spoon. Lower 7 to 8 inches of both ends of the wick into the wax. After one minute, lift the wick out.

**5.** As the wax cools, straighten the entire length of each coated end of the wick with your fingers. This is called priming the wick and should be done after each dipping to keep your candles smooth and even.

**6.** Hang the wick over your drying rack for at least 1 minute to let the wax harden. Don't be disappointed at how skinny your candles look; it takes 30 to 40 dippings to make good candles.

**7.** Dip the wick again, for just 3 seconds this time. Prime the wick and place it on the hardening rack for 1 minute.

**8.** Repeat step 7 until your candles look finished. It will take at least 30 dippings. *Note: Make sure the water does not cook out of the pot. Add more water as needed, but don't let water get into the wax.*

**9.** Have the adult raise the temperature of the wax to 180°F and do two final dippings at 3 seconds each. This will give your candles a smooth finish. After the final dipping, leave the candles on the rack for about 2 hours.

**10.** With scissors, trim the wicks to a length of about ½ inch. To trim the base of the candles, ask the adult to heat a paring knife in hot water for easier cutting and then trim.

**11.** Wait 24 hours before having an adult light your candles.

# Advances in Lighting

People have used electric lights for only a little more than 100 years. Before electricity, candles were the basic source of night lighting. In the 1750s, Benjamin Franklin designed the first street lights in colonial America. About 20 lamps, burning whale oil, were installed in Franklin's city of Philadelphia.

In addition to dipping candles, the colonists began using candle molds late in the colonial period. They used iron or tin molds to make eight or more candles at the same time. In the 1800s, candle makers used molds to make candles in all sorts of shapes, like clowns and animals.

# SPATTERWORK
# CLAY CANDLESTICK

The colonists made candleholders from a wide variety of materials, including clay, tin, pewter, and brass. The simplest candlesticks were made of clay. Colonists took most of their handmade clay items to a village potter who fired them in a special oven called a kiln. This turned the clay into hard pottery that could be used to hold food or liquids. Clay candlesticks were often simply dried in the sun rather than a kiln.

For your candlestick, you can use self-hardening clay, available in craft and hobby stores. To decorate it, you'll use a painting technique called spatterwork.

## MATERIALS

*several sheets of newspaper*
*1-pound package of self-hardening clay*
*rolling pin or round bottle*
*ruler*
*round drinking glass, about 5 inches in diameter*
    *(An empty tin can will also work.)*
*old table knife*
*2 or more craft sticks*
*candle*
*medium paintbrush, about ½ inch*
*poster paints or acrylic paints: white and one other*
    *color of your choice*
*old cardboard carton (optional)*

*small dish or paper cup*
*tap water*
*old toothbrush*

**1.** Spread the newspaper on your work surface.

**2.** Read the directions on the package of clay. Remove the clay from the package and work it with your hands to make it soft and easy to shape.

**3.** Flatten the block of clay with the heel of your hands and with your fingers. Then use the rolling pin (or bottle) to roll it out and flatten it more, until it looks like a pancake and measures about ⅜ inch thick (a little less than ½ an inch thick).

**4.** Press the glass into the clay to make a circle about 5 inches in diameter (across). Push the glass all the way through the clay so you can lift out the circle. This will be the base of your candlestick.

**5.** Use an old table knife to cut off 4 to 5 thin strands from the leftover flattened-out clay that measure ½ inch wide each. To make the side of the candleholder (about ½ inch high), place a strand of clay around the top of the base, as shown. If the strand doesn't reach all the way around the base, add more strands as needed. Smooth the seam between the side and the base with a craft stick. You can add a little wet clay to make sure the side sticks to the base.

**6.** To form a candleholder, cut off another strand of clay ¾ inch wide and just long enough to wrap around your candle. Form the strand into a circle and place it in the center of the base. Use a little wet clay to stick the holder to the base; then use a table knife or craft stick to smooth the seam.

**7.** Add a handle with another strand of clay. Fix it firmly to the top of the base and to the side of the base, as shown in the drawing. *Note: This handle is only for decoration. Don't try to carry the candlestick by the handle.*

**8.** When all the seams are smooth, allow the candlestick to dry completely. (Read the package directions to see how long the clay takes to dry, or allow the clay to dry overnight.)

**9.** Use a medium paintbrush to coat the entire candlestick with white paint. Allow the paint to dry. Apply a second coat, if necessary.

**10.** Before spattering the paint, make sure you

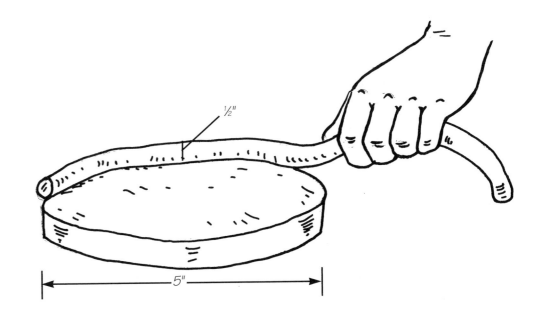

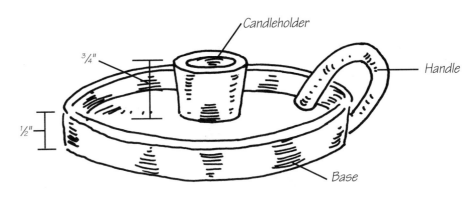

have plenty of newspaper covering your work surface. Add extra if necessary. Optional: Place your candlestick in an old cardboard carton to control the spattering even more.

# From Candlesticks to Chandeliers

Colonial craftworkers made beautiful candlesticks out of materials like silver, pewter, brass, and glass. They also made very elaborate chandeliers, holding twenty or more candles, for churches, public meeting places, and the homes of wealthier colonists. Many of these beautifully designed pieces can be seen today in museums and in buildings from colonial times.

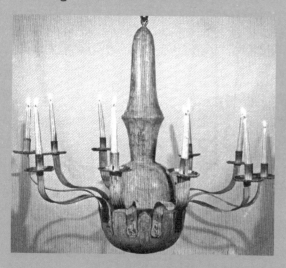

**11.** Pour a little of the color you've chosen into a small dish or paper cup, and add a few drops of water.

**12.** Dip an old toothbrush into the paint. Hold the brush in one hand, about 6 inches from the candlestick. With the other hand, slowly run a craft stick over the bristles crossways, pulling the stick toward you, so that the paint spatters onto the candlestick and not you. Turn the candlestick to cover all areas with spatterwork, letting as much of the white show through as you wish. When the paint is dry, your candlestick is ready.

# WINTER FUN

Early in December, Sarah and Nathan used their new weather wisdom to predict the first major storm of the winter. The storm lasted two days and left a deep blanket of snow that came up to the children's knees. With other children in the village, they made Iroquois snow snakes and had contests to see whose snake would slide farthest down a snow-packed slope.

A few days after the storm, the sky was clear blue. The sun was so bright on the snow that it was hard to look at anything. Mr. Mayhew showed the children how to make snow goggles to protect their eyes from the glare. He had learned about snow goggles from a trader named Little Rain, a member of the Penobscot tribe that lived in northern New England.

On days when Sarah, Nathan, and the twins could play in the snow, they usually came home wet and cold. Mrs. Mayhew fixed steaming mugs of hot chocolate, while the children warmed and dried themselves in front of the fire. If their work was done for the day, they could then play indoor games like jackstraws.

## PROJECT · THE GAME OF JACKSTRAWS

The modern game we know as pick-up sticks is the same game the colonists called jackstraws or spillikin. Colonial children and adults played this game of skill and concentration, usually using straws or twigs. Wealthier colonists bought fancier sets made of polished bone or ivory. You can play the game the way colonial children did by using straws from a broom. Take straws from an old broom or buy broom straw at a craft or hobby store. When you become skilled at jackstraws, you can make the game more difficult by adding 10 or 20 more straws.

### MATERIALS

*scissors*

*21 broom straws (You can also use thin sticks or dowels.)*

*ruler*

*2 or more players*

**1.** To make the game: Use the scissors to trim off any side pieces from the straws. Cut the straws to a length of 6 inches.

**2.** To start:

**a.** Player 1 holds the bunch of straws with the fingertips of one hand at the top of the straws. The bottom of the straws must rest on the playing surface.

**b.** The player suddenly lets go of the straws so that they land in a jumbled heap.

**3.** To play:

**a.** Player 1 tries to lift one straw off the pile without disturbing any of the others. If she succeeds without moving any other straw, she keeps that straw and tries for another. But if she moves any straw accidentally, her turn is over and the straw she was picking up goes back on the pile.

**b.** The game continues until all the straws have been picked up. Each player keeps the straws that he or she has picked up. As long as a player lifts a straw without moving others, she can keep going.

**4.** To win: When all the straws have been picked up, the player with the most straws is the winner.

# PROJECT · ALGONQUIN SNOW GOGGLES

The Algonquin tribes had a special way of protecting their eyes from the glare of the sun on snow. They made snow goggles with very narrow slits for the eyes. The Algonquins may have learned to make these from the Eskimo and Aleut peoples who lived farther north, and the Algonquins, in turn, taught the colonists.

Both the Algonquins and the colonists made their snow goggles out of birch bark or thin pieces of wood. You can make very similar goggles using stiff cardboard. You'll find they're useful when the sun reflects brightly off water or sand, as well as snow. Try your goggles on any extra-bright day. Once you get used to looking through the slits, you'll be surprised at how much better you can see. Remember, though, never to look directly at the sun, as it can damage your eyes.

## MATERIALS
*3-by-6-inch piece of stiff cardboard or heavy-gauge*
*poster board*
*pencil*
*ruler*
*scissors*
*old magazine or cutting board*
*craft knife (to be handled by an adult)*
*several sheets of newspaper*
*small paintbrush*
*black poster paint*
*stapler*
*12-inch strip of elastic (available in the sewing*
*section of stores) or string*
*adult helper*

**1.** Ask the adult helper to hold the cardboard up to your face, as if you were measuring to make a Halloween mask. If the cardboard is too wide for your face, trim a little off each side with scissors. The helper should use the pencil to draw two lines, each about 1½ inches wide, one in front of each of your eyes.

**2.** Cut out a small triangle so the goggles will fit over your nose.

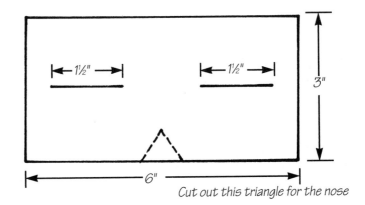

*Cut out this triangle for the nose*

# Snowshoes: Another Native American Invention

Native Americans of several tribes, including the Penobscot, Aleut, and Eskimo, developed snowshoes to make it easier to travel long distances on snow. They bent the wood of ash trees or willow trees to make the curved front, then tied rawhide in a crisscross pattern to make the platform. Hunters and messengers could travel with remarkable speed on oval-shaped snowshoes, which they called bear paws.

**3.** Lay the goggles flat on an old magazine or cutting board. Use the pencil and ruler to draw outlines for two eye slits around the 1½-inch lines you drew. Each slit should be about 1½ inches wide and ¼ inch high.

**4.** Ask the adult to use the craft knife to cut out the two slits.

**5.** Spread the newspaper on your work surface. With the paint brush, paint one side of the goggles with a coat of black paint. Let the paint dry for about 15 minutes, then paint the other side and the edges of the slits. Let the paint dry for another 15 minutes.

**6.** Use the stapler to attach one end of the 12-inch strip of elastic to one side of the goggles. Staple the elastic twice, as shown.

**7.** Place the goggles against your face to see how long the elastic should be for a comfortable fit. Cut off any extra elastic. Staple the loose end to the other side of the goggles, again stapling twice. If you use string instead of elastic, cut the string into two pieces. Staple one end of each piece of string to either side of the goggles. Ask your helper to tie the other two string ends at the back of your head. Your goggles are now ready.

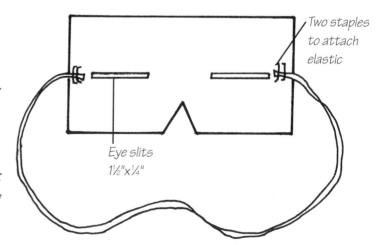

Two staples to attach elastic

Eye slits 1½"x¼"

# PROJECT IROQUOIS SNOW SNAKES

This game is believed to have been invented by the people of the Iroquois nation who lived in New York colony. Iroquois men played the game with beautifully carved sticks about 10 feet long. Native American and colonial children used shorter sticks, like you'll be doing.

Although the game was designed to be played down a chute of hard-packed snow, it can also be played on ice, on the hard sand of a beach, or even on grass. Work with one or more friends on this project so you can have contests to see whose snow snake can go the farthest.

## MATERIALS
*2 or more old broomsticks or mop handles, each*
  *about 4 feet long (You'll need one stick for each*
  *player. You can also use ¼ round molding or dowels*
  *available at lumber supply stores.)*
*permanent marking pens: black and any other colors*
  *of your choice*
*rag*
*furniture wax*
*2 or more players*

**1.** To make the snakes:
**a.** Choose one side of the stick to be the head. (If your stick has a rounded part, that should be the head.) Use black marking pen to make two eyes and a mouth.
**b.** Decorate the rest of your snow snake with colorful stripes, dots, or any design you wish. Draw a tail on your snake. Each snow snake should have a special look.
**c.** Use a rag to apply a coat of furniture wax to the entire snow snake. This will protect the drawings and give the snake a little extra speed.

**2.** To set up a hurling track:
**a.** Find a clear outdoor area, either on level ground or sloping down a hill.
**b.** If you're playing on snow, make a groove or chute about 2 feet wide and 6 to 10 inches deep. Pack the snow firmly to make a faster track. On sand or grass, mark off a hurling track with stones or twigs, about 6 feet wide.
**c.** Mark a starting line with your foot.
**d.** Practice hurling a snow snake to see how long the track should be. Make the track a little longer than the farthest practice throw.

**3.** To play:
**a.** Hurl a snow snake underhand. Grip the snake by the tip of the tail and let the head rest on the ground. Then shove the snake down the track, as

if you were launching a sled. You can use your other hand to balance the snake if necessary, but you must keep the snake close to the ground, not in the air.

**b.** Each player takes a turn sending his snow snake down the track. The player who throws his snake the farthest scores one point. A round is played when each player throws his snake once. Any player who throws a snow snake through the air loses a turn.

**4.** To win: The first player to score 10 points wins the game.

# AFTERNOON PROJECTS

On days when it was too cold to be outside, all of the Mayhews would gather in the common room. While a roast slowly cooked over the fire, they spent the afternoon working on different projects.

Mrs. Mayhew was making an appliqué quilt. She cut scraps of fabric into the shape of different farm animals, then sewed them onto larger squares. She planned to take the squares to the next quilting bee to sew them together, add the backing, and fill the quilt with a layer of warm, soft goose feathers.

Sarah was making pomander balls by sticking cloves in oranges and lemons, then coating the fruit with spices. The pomanders looked pretty when they were tied with a ribbon and, like potpourri, they provided a pleasant scent. Nathan worked on a Mohawk bead necklace, drilling holes in bear claws and bits of bone.

And the whole family worked together to decorate the common room with stencils. Mrs. Mayhew

had designed the stencils, drawing graceful flowers, leaves, and vines. Mr. Mayhew cut the stencils out of thin pieces of tin, and everyone in the family, even the twins, had fun painting with the stencils.

The Mayhews enjoyed their winter projects, but sometimes the children would gaze out the window and wonder when the spring thaw would begin. They talked about picking wild berries again, and Sarah was already planning her kitchen garden.

# PROJECT STENCILED NOTE CARDS

Stencils are pieces of paper or stiff material that have designs or letters cut out of them. You paint over the stencil, onto another surface. Stenciling allows you to use the same design over and over.

In this project, you'll use stencils to make a set of six colorful note cards. You can copy one of the designs shown here, create your own, or copy a pattern from a book on stenciling in the library. You can buy special stencil paper and a stencil brush at hobby, craft, or art supply stores, but thin cardboard and a paintbrush with stiff bristles will work just as well. Once you see how much fun stenciling is, you can stencil lots of things, like book covers or a wooden box. Use your note cards to write and mail messages or short letters.

## MATERIALS

*scissors*
*three 8½-by-11-inch sheets of white paper*
*6 standard-size white envelopes, 3 5/8 inches*
   *x 6½ inches*
*pencil*
*ruler*
*4-by-6-inch piece of thin cardboard (File folders*
   *work well.)*
*old magazine or cutting board*
*craft knife (to be handled only by an adult)*
*several sheets of newspaper*

*acrylic paints or poster paints: 3 colors of your choice*
*3 small dishes or plastic cups*
*masking tape*
*stencil brush or small paintbrush with stiff bristles*
*paper towels*
*black felt-tip pen with fine point*
*adult helper*

**1.** Use the scissors to cut one of the sheets of paper in half. Fold each half-sheet over to make the shape of a note card.

**2.** Use the ruler to measure the envelope. Measure your note cards and trim the bottom of each one so that it will fit easily into the envelope.

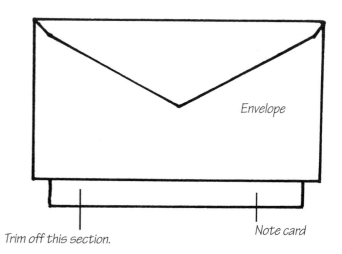

*Envelope*

*Trim off this section.*

*Note card*

**3.** Repeat steps 1 and 2 with the other two sheets of paper to make a total of 6 blank cards.

**4.** To make the stencil, copy either the drawing of the sailing ship or the tulip and birds onto the thin piece of cardboard.

*Designs for stencils*

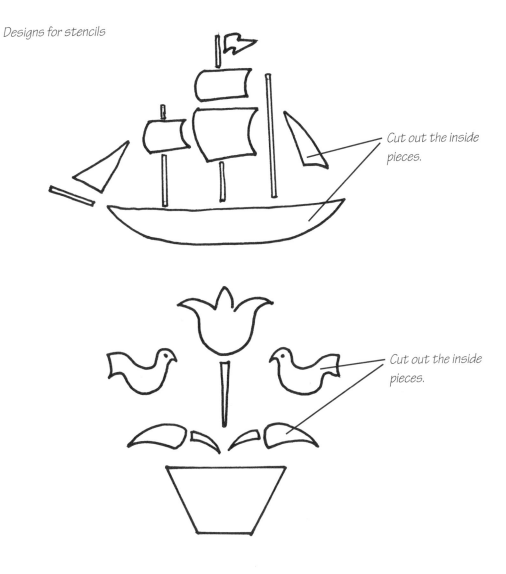

*Cut out the inside pieces.*

*Cut out the inside pieces.*

# Colonial Stencil Art

In colonial times, people used stencils in many different ways. They stenciled walls to make them look like the expensive wallpaper that wealthy colonists imported from France. Some colonists even stenciled their floors to imitate the carpets of the well-to-do. They also applied stencils to furniture, clock cases, and all sorts of boxes. Traveling painters called limners would stencil homes or churches in exchange for a room and meals.

**5.** Place the cardboard on an old magazine or cutting board. Ask the adult to use the craft knife to cut out the stencil pieces from the cardboard.

**6.** Spread the sheets of newspaper on your work surface. Pour a little of each of the paint colors you've chosen into its own small dish or plastic cup.

**7.** Place your stencil over the center of one of the note cards. Use 3 or 4 pieces of masking tape to hold the stencil in place.

**8.** Holding your stencil brush vertically, dip the tip into the paint. You need very little paint, so tap off the excess on a paper towel.

**9.** Still holding the brush straight, brush it over the stencil opening, moving from the edge of the opening and painting toward the middle.

**10.** Rinse the brush, dry it on a paper towel, and apply another color the same way. When you finish painting with all 3 colors, carefully lift off the stencil. Let the paint dry for about 20 minutes.

**11.** When the paint is dry, add any details, like the birds' eyes or ropes on the ship with the black felt-tip pen.

**12.** Repeat steps 7 through 11 with the other 5 blank cards. You're now ready to use your note cards.

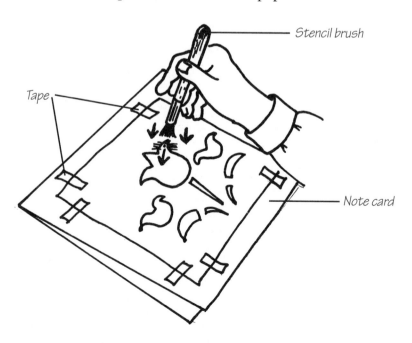

Stencil brush

Tape

Note card

# PROJECT APPLIQUÉ PICTURE

Appliqué is sort of like painting with fabric. You cut small pieces of fabric into shapes, then apply or appliqué them to a background cloth. Because cloth was both expensive and time consuming to make, the colonists saved every scrap to use for projects like appliquéd quilts.

Colonial women sewed the scraps onto the background, but you can create an attractive picture using felt and glue. Either copy the picture shown of a colonial girl bringing home a stray sheep, or create your own appliqué scene. If you don't have scraps of felt at home, you can buy them at any fabric or department store.

## MATERIALS

*several sheets of newspaper*
*10-by-6-inch piece of light green felt*
*10-by-3-inch piece of light blue felt*
*4 or 5 straight pins*
*pencil*
*scissors*
*10-by-6-inch piece of stiff cardboard*
*craft glue or white glue*
*craft stick or scrap of stiff cardboard*
*scraps of felt: yellow, white, brown, dark green,*
  *gray, and pink*
*black ballpoint pen*
*4 thumbtacks or transparent tape (optional)*

**1.** Spread the newspaper on your work surface..

**2.** To shape the ground and sky, lay the piece of light green felt on the work surface. Place the light blue strip of felt over the upper part of the green strip so the two pieces overlap. Use 4 or 5 straight pins to pin the two pieces together.

**3.** Draw an uneven pencil line across the blue strip where it overlaps the green. This will give you a realistic looking horizon, as shown in the picture.

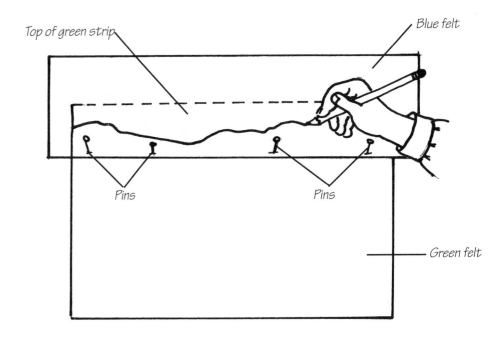

Top of green strip

Blue felt

Pins

Pins

Green felt

**4.** Use the scissors to cut along the pencil line through both pieces of fabric. The blue sky strip will now match up with the green along the horizon. Remove the pins.

**5.** Lay the 10-inch-by-6-inch piece of cardboard on the work surface. Position the blue and green pieces on the cardboard so the edges fit together.

**6.** Spread glue thinly and evenly on the back of each piece of felt and glue it to the cardboard backing. Use a craft stick or a scrap of stiff cardboard to help you spread the glue. (Remember to keep the glue thin so it doesn't show through the fabric.)

**7.** Copy the objects shown in the picture by drawing each one on a felt scrap with pencil. Cut small strips of brown felt to make the fence. You can draw and cut out other felt objects if you wish, like birds or flowers.

**8.** When you have cut out all the pieces, position them on the picture. Use the arrangement shown here, or place the objects any way you like.

**9.** Apply a thin coat of glue to the back of each piece and fix it in place.

**10.** Use the black ballpoint pen to add details, like the girl's feet, the sheep's eye, and the rope.

**11.** With adult permission, you can hang your appliqué picture on a wall with thumbtacks or loops of transparent tape.

yellow

white

gray

light blue

dark brown

dark green

brown

brown

brown

light green

white

pink

6"

10"

# PROJECT POMANDER BALL

The colonists used pomander balls much like sachets or potpourris. They were especially useful for clearing the air of the heavy odors caused by cooking in an open fireplace. Pomander balls remain popular today. Many people hang them from their Christmas trees, so that the spicy aroma mixes with the pine scent of the tree. Pomanders are easy and fun to make, and if you work with a partner, you can make several to give as gifts.

## MATERIALS

*several paper towels*

*masking tape, ¼ or ½ inch wide*

*1 medium-size orange*

*medium-size nail*

*about 30 whole cloves*

*paper towels*

*double sheet of tissue paper or 3 paper towels*

*measuring spoon*

*1 tablespoon ground cinnamon*

*1 tablespoon ground nutmeg*

*1 tablespoon allspice*

*1 tablespoon ground orrisroot (optional), available at craft stores, natural food stores, and some supermarkets*

*small mixing spoon or teaspoon*

*two ½-by-18-inch pieces of narrow cloth ribbon, any color*

*adult helper*

**1.** Spread several paper towels over your work surface.

**2.** Wrap a piece of masking tape all the way around the orange. Wrap a second piece around the orange in the other direction, as shown in the picture. (The tape will form a path for the ribbon you'll use to hang the pomander ball.)

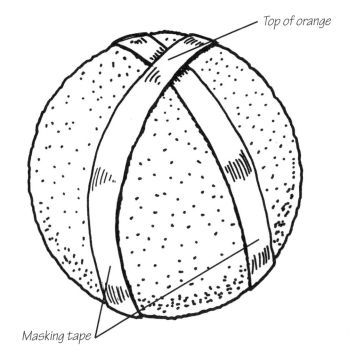

Top of orange

Masking tape

**3.** Ask the adult to help you use a nail to poke about 20 holes through the skin of the orange—but not through the tape. The holes should be spread evenly around the whole orange.

**4.** Push at least 30 whole cloves into the skin of the orange. (They don't have to form any pattern.) If the skin is too thick, ask the adult to help you use the nail to start a hole for each clove. Don't stick the cloves through the holes you made in step 3 or through the tape.

**5.** Remove the masking tape. Wipe off the orange—and your hands—with damp paper towels.

**6.** Spread a double sheet of tissue paper (or 3 paper towels) on your work surface.

Measure the cinnamon, nutmeg, and allspice onto the tissue paper.

**7.** [optional] Add ground orrisroot to the spices. (Orrisroot is a substance that will make the aroma last longer.)

**8.** Use the small spoon to mix the spices together on the tissue paper.

**9.** Roll the orange around in the spice mixture. Use your fingers to poke some of the mixture into the holes you made in step 3.

**10.** Wrap the orange in the tissue paper and store it in a cool, dark place for 2 to 3 weeks. As it dries, the orange will shrink a little and the skin will harden. This change is called "curing." When the skin feels hard, the pomander is ready.

**11.** Wind a piece of ribbon around the pomander ball along the paths left by the tape. Cross the ribbon at the bottom, then tie a double knot and a bow at the top, as shown.

**12.** Slide the second ribbon under the double knot and form it into a long loop for hanging. Tie a double knot and a bow at the top of the loop, as shown.

## PROJECT

# MOHAWK BEAD NECKLACE

Native Americans in almost every tribe made necklaces out of a wide variety of materials, including animal claws and bones, shells, and bits of stone. They bored holes through the objects and strung them on rawhide. Native American women often made their necklaces out of just beads and shells. Some men, like the warriors of the Mohawk tribe of the Iroquois nation, used a combination of claws and other items.

The necklace you'll make out of self-hardening clay is based on the Mohawk style. The result is a handsome piece that can be worn by a boy or girl, or it can be hung as a wall decoration.

## MATERIALS

*several sheets of newspaper*
*1-pound package of self-hardening clay*
*ruler*
*old table knife or craft stick*
*large nail or knitting needle*
*small paintbrush*
*acrylic paints: dark brown, white, and any other*
 *colors you choose*
*20-inch rawhide lace (sold as shoelaces), or twine*
*adult helper*

**1.** Spread the newspaper over your work surface.

**2.** Open the package of self-hardening clay and knead it with your hands to make it softer and easy to shape.

**3.** Pull off a small piece of clay and form it into the shape of a bear claw about 1½ inches long and less than ¼ inch thick, as shown in the picture on page 108. Use the old table knife or craft stick to help you shape the clay. Ask an adult to help you use a large nail or knitting needle to make a hole in the upper part of the claw for stringing.

**4.** Repeat step 3 to make four more claws. Set the claws aside to dry.

**5.** Pull off another small piece of clay and roll it with your fingers and palms into a long, thin rope, about ⅜ inch thick. Use the table knife to cut off a piece of the rope about ¾ inch long. Ask an adult to help you carefully push a nail or knitting needle through the clay the long way to make a hollow tube, as shown.

**6.** Repeat step 5 to make three more of these hollow bone pieces.

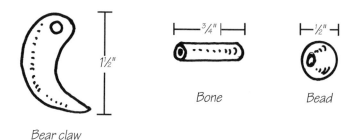

1½"

¾"

½"

Bear claw

Bone

Bead

low, and blue, to paint the beads for a striking contrast to the bear claws and bones.

**11.** Allow the paint to dry for 20 to 30 minutes.

**12.** When the paint is dry, run the piece of rawhide lacing or twine through each of the holes. Arrange the items in the pattern shown in the picture.

**13.** Tie the ends of the rawhide in a tight double knot, and your Mohawk necklace is ready to wear.

**7.** Break off a small piece of clay and form it with your fingers into a round ball, about ½ inch thick. Again, have an adult help you make a hole through the ball to make a round bead for stringing.

**8.** Repeat step 7 to make nine more beads.

**9.** Allow all the clay pieces to dry completely. (Read the directions on the package of clay to see how long the drying takes.)

**10.** Use the small paintbrush and acrylic paints to paint each of the necklace items. (You might find it useful to hold each item on the nail or knitting needle when you paint so you can paint all the way around.) The bear claws should be dark brown and the bones should be white. Use different bright colors, like red, yel-

# GLOSSARY

**Algonquin**    A group of Native American tribes who lived on the east coast of what is now the United States and Canada.

**American Revolution** (1775–1783)    The war the American colonies fought against England, which resulted in their independence and the establishment of the United States as a nation.

**apothecary**    A person who sold medicines and drugs, like a modern pharmacist.

**appliqué**    A sewing technique that involves sewing patches of different shapes onto a background fabric.

**apprentice**    A person who is learning a trade or business by working with a person skilled in that field.

**barometer**    A tool used to predict changes in weather by measuring air pressure.

**bee**    A group working session that was also a social occasion in colonial times, such as quilting bees and flaxing bees. Same as a frolic.

**carding**    The process of straightening fibers of wool with a stiff wire brush, or card, before spinning the fibers into yarn.

**cattail**    A tall plant that grows in marshes and swamps with a sausage-shaped seed head containing hundreds of tiny seeds.

**churn**    A wooden or pottery container, with a paddle built into the lid, used to stir, or churn, cream to make butter.

**colony**    A territory in a distant land settled by a group of people who continue to be governed by the parent country.

**common room**    The main room of a colonial home, used for cooking, eating, working, and relaxing.

**cure**    To change a substance by storing it for a period of time.

**dye bath**    A mixture of plant dye and hot water used to dye cloth.

**dyestuff**    The plant material used for dyeing fabric.

**endpapers**    The inside covers of a book.

**enfleurage**    A process of making perfume by combining fats and oils with the scent of fresh flowers.

**fixative**    An ingredient used to fix, or hold, a dye color in fabric, and also to make aroma last longer.

**flax**    A plant with slender stems used to make linen thread and cloth.

**flaxbrake**    A wooden tool used to pound flax to soften it for making linen.

**frolic**    A group working session that was also a social occasion. Same as a bee.

**furrows**    Rows plowed in a farm field for planting seeds.

**gnomon**    The upright part of a sundial.

**gus-to-weh ("real hat")**    Algonquin word for a hat of soft deerskin, decorated with feathers.

**harrow**    To break up the large clumps of soil after a farm field has been plowed.

**hob**    The stake used as a target in a game of quoits.

**indigo**    A plant grown in warm climates used to make a blue dye that was very popular in colonial times.

**Iroquois**    A powerful nation of five Native American tribes living in the New York colony.

**jackstraws**    Also called "spillikin," the colonial name for the game known today as pick-up sticks.

**joiner**    A colonial carpenter.

**journeyman**    A colonial craftsperson who moved from place to place selling his or her skills. Both men and women could be journeymen.

**kiln**    A special oven used to heat clay objects at very high temperatures to harden them into pottery.

**lard**    The fat of a pig, used by the colonists as a shortening in cooking and to make soap.

**limner**    A colonial craftsperson skilled in stencil painting.

**loom**  A frame used for weaving.

**maple water**  European colonist's name for the sap from the maple trees.

**marbling**  The process of creating a marbled design on paper.

**Mohawk**  One of the tribes of the Iroquois nation in the New York colony.

**Mohegan**  One of the Algonquin tribes of New England, known for their friendliness to the early colonists.

**mordant bath**  A mixture used to fix the color when dyeing fabric.

**nib**  The point of a pen, or the tip of a quill pen.

**paraffin wax**  A product developed around 1870 to replace tallow in candles.

**peel**  A long wooden paddle used for placing bread or pies into a fireplace oven.

**plantation**  A large farm in the Southern colonies.

**pomander ball**  An orange, lemon, or lime studded with cloves and cured with spices to use as an air freshener.

**pomme**  French word for "apple."

**potpourri**  Mixture of dried herbs, spices, and flower petals used to sweeten the air, sometimes in a sachet.

**print butter**  Butter that has had a design pressed into it with a butter mold.

**quick bread**    Bread made without yeast so no waiting time is needed for the dough to rise.

**quill**    Hollow spiny shaft of a feather or the feather itself.

**quoits**    A colonial game similar to horseshoes but played with circular rings.

**rawhide**    The hide or leather of deer, cattle, or other animals.

**ringer**    When a quoit encircles the hob, or stake, in a game of quoits.

**sachet**    A small cloth bag filled with potpourri and used to add a pleasant aroma to rooms and storage areas.

**shuttle**    A small, flat tool used in weaving to weave the weft threads in and out of the warp.

**skein**    A length of yarn wound into a coil.

**slump**    A cooling colonial dessert made with bread and fruit.

**snow snake**    A Native American and colonial game in which decorated sticks are hurled down a snow-packed track.

**spatterwork**    A painting technique of splattering paint on an object rather than brushing.

**spiles**    Hollow spouts tapped into maple trees to draw out the maple sap.

**spillikin**    Also called "jackstraws," a colonial name for a game known today as pick-up sticks.

**spring house** A house built over a spring used for keeping foods cool in warm weather and protecting them from freezing in winter.

**stencil** A stiff material with a design or picture cut out of it, used to paint repeated copies.

**stick toss game** A game played by most Native American tribes, using animal rib bones with painted designs.

**sugaring off** The last stage in boiling down maple sap to make maple syrup.

**sundial** An instrument that shows the time of day by the shadow of a gnomon on a surface.

**swingling knife** A tool used to clean the flax fibers for making linen.

**syllabub** A foamy colonial drink made with fruit juice and milk or cream.

**tallow** Animal fat used in making candles.

**warp** The first threads placed on a loom to form a base for weaving.

**weather vane** A thin wooden or metal plate, often carved in the shape of an animal, that pivots on a pole to show wind direction.

**weft** In weaving, the threads that are woven in and out of the warp to create a weave.

# BIBLIOGRAPHY

Suzanne I. Barchers and Patricia C. Marden. *Cooking Up U.S. History: Recipes and Research to Share with Children.* Chicago: Teachers Ideas Press, 1991.

Josef and Dorothy Berger, eds. *Diary of America.* New York: Simon & Schuster, 1957.

*Cobblestone, The History Magazine for Young People.* 30 Grove Street, Peterborough, NH 03458.
    *Old Sturbridge Village,* Feb. 1982
    *Children's Toys,* Dec. 1986
    *The People of Williamsburg,* Feb. 1990
    *Colonial Craftsmen,* June 1990
    *America's Folk Art,* Aug. 1991

Marshall Davidson. *Life in America,* 2 vols. Boston: Houghton Mifflin, 1951.

David C. King. *America's Story, Book I: Colonial America, 1600-1750.* Littleton, MA: Sundance, 1996.

Jean Lipman and Alice Winchester. *The Flowering of American Folk Art, 1776-1876.* Philadelphia: Running Press, 1987.

Nina Fletcher Little. *Country Art in Early American Homes.* New York: E. P. Dutton & Co., 1975.

Allan and Paulette Macfarlan. *Handbook of American Indian Games.* New York: Dover Publications, 1985.

Bernard S. Mason. *How to Make Drums, Tomtoms and Rattles.* New York: Dover Publications, 1974.

Marz and Nono Minor. *The American Indian Craft Book.* Lincoln, NE: University of Nebraska Press, 1972.

William Wells Newell. *Games and Songs of American Children.* New York: Harper and Brothers, 1903; reprinted by Dover Publications, 1963.

Eric Sloane. *Diary of an Early American Boy.* New York: Random House, 1965.

Marlene Smith-Baranzini and Howard Egger Bovet. *Book of the New American Nation.* Brown Paper School U. S. Kids History. Boston: Little, Brown, 1995.

Elizabeth Stenson. *Early Settler Activity Guide.* New York: Crabtree, 1992.

# INDEX